Grounded Faith for Practical People

The Simple Visual Guide to Confident Faith

MIKE TAYLOR

mikeptaylor.net

Cover design: Humberto Amaro

Cover photo credit: stock.adobe.com

Illustrations designed by Mike Taylor

Photo credits: unsplash.com, pexels.com, pixabay.com, stock.adobe.com, canva.com, and commons.wikipedia.org

Dedicated to Sydney, Jackson, and Nora Paige.

"The ideas I stand for are not mine. I borrowed them from Socrates. I swiped them from Chesterfield. I stole them from Jesus. And I put them in a book. If you don't like their rules whose would you use?"

- DALE CARNEGIE

Table of Contents

Preface

If you're reading this, it means that you're hungry. You're hungry for more, hungry for something, hungry for *anything* real.

I know because I've been there, and in a lot of ways, I believe it's good to stay there. Some people would tell you that there's a period in your life for searching, but I believe we're at our healthiest when we're searching. Not searching from a place of skepticism or insecurity, but searching for the simple fact that what you've already found is so incredible, and there's always more. In that regard, seeking is a lifelong endeavor.

What's unique about this book is that I wrote it a little at a time as I was going through an incredibly uncomfortable, and at times painful, process of discovery. I don't, however, believe that this information is only for people who are going through a process of discovery. As a matter of fact, as I read back through these pages, it only strengthens what I've found to be true regarding faith. Therefore, I believe this is evergreen information. You never outgrow it, and it never gets old.

We never reach a place where we don't need to be reminded of our roots. From time to time, everyone doubts their beliefs. That's what humans do. We have flaws, and we're faulty; therefore, we doubt even the things we know to be true. That's where the information in these pages can help.

Whether you're searching for the first time or you're firm in your beliefs, this book will give you a more stable stance regardless of your place on the journey.

I want you to know up front that I am not a scientist or a theologian. I'm a writer, and that's what I do best. I research and write and simplify the convoluted. Through my journey of doubt and searching for answers, I found a lot of information. So much so, that it took me years to weed through it all.

As I began to take notes and write down the things that I was learning, I realized there was a need for simplification. After all, I figured there had to be other people who were either searching or simply wanted more confidence in the beliefs they were already living out.

That's what this book is. It's a compilation and summation of the facts that make up the foundation of the Christian faith. I believe the information in this book is what makes up the faith of any person who is strong in their beliefs. After all, faith is based on information, and my goal for this book is to simplify otherwise complicated information in a way that you can actually apply and use in your everyday life.

In other words, whether you're facing an existential crisis, doubting the beliefs you've had your entire life, or simply having a bad day, my hope is that you will use this book as a quick visual resource for building and reinforcing confidence in your beliefs.

Although *I'm* not a scientist or theologian, all the information in this book has come from such sources. I believe that we're all at least somewhat of a compilation of the people we've had the privilege of looking up to, so I have no problem admitting that most of the ideas in this book did not originate with me. Instead, they're my interpretation and simplification of ideas that existed long before I discovered them.

If you're skeptical, I get it. Everyone's skeptical. Church people are skeptical. Atheists are skeptical. Republicans and Democrats, capitalists and socialists - they're all equally skeptical. We're all skeptical. The true way forward is to open your mind enough to let the possibility of a new idea come in. If it doesn't add up, choose not to believe it and file it away.

But don't box yourself into your comfort zone because you're too afraid of what you might find outside of it. After all, the best things in life are usually located on the other side of the things that make us most uncomfortable.

Please do yourself a favor and do not write off this information as something you either already know or don't need. Facts are facts, and if you're willing to follow those facts to wherever they lead you, then I believe by the end of this book, you will reach a place of incredible hope and confidence.

That's the purpose of this book, and that's my hope for you - that your eyes would be opened to a worldview bigger than anything you previously thought possible.

Going Through the Motions

Do you feel like you're just going through the motions? Maybe you've found yourself caught in the same routine day in and day out without confidence and passion about why you're alive. Maybe you just wish you had a stronger sense of purpose. Maybe you actually want to be confident in your beliefs so that you're not shaken by every doubt you experience.

We all have beliefs that make us feel safe and comfortable, but too many people avoid truly *believing* anything. We live in a world of avoidance and middle grounds. We avoid the most difficult questions in life and dodge our doubts by sticking with safe answers.

Pew Research found that 9 out of 10 people in America believe that there is a God or at least a "higher power." Yet only 28% of people say they talk to God, and God talks to them, and only 27% of people believe God is in control of their life all the time.[1]

In other words, almost everyone knows there's *something* or *someone* out there, and some of us call Him God, but very few people actually trust or live connected to the one *true* loving God.

That's a serious problem, and it's exactly why most of us experience a chaotic internal existence with little to no genuine peace. This applies to both religious and non-religious people. It's also no coincidence that at the same time, our society is experiencing an increase in mental illness cases and suicide.[2]

Most live in a state of internal turmoil, and this is the root of the problem we face:

We know that at the very least, there *should* be a God, but we're not connected to the one *true* God in a real way because we lack the confidence to do so.

Too many of us either convince ourselves that God isn't really there or that He's distant and uninvolved. Both of these worldviews lead to hopelessness at some point in our lives. The good news is, both of these worldviews are untrue.

I believe too many of us keep God in our minds as a crutch – something that makes us feel good – rather than our source of life.

Religious people love the idea of God because it makes them feel better when they do the "right" things and when other people do the "wrong" things.

"Spiritual" people love the idea of there being something bigger than themselves out there; they just don't want to commit to Him because they're afraid He might ask for something in return if they did.

People who claim not to believe in God at all actually believe in God; they just don't label him as such. They call God names like "science" or "the universe" or "nature" or whatever label makes them feel comfortable. They use these labels because they think they don't have to address something they won't acknowledge.

The problem, of course, is that none of these views are true. Truth is based on the accumulation of evidence which establishes facts, and all three of these worldviews go against the evidence that supports a loving Creator.

The truth is, almost everyone is on the fence; most people just won't say it out loud. In this book, I want to show you a different path - one based on facts - that doesn't lead you to a mundane life based on what makes us feel good, which so many of us are leading.

I want you to be confident in your purpose and reason for existence, and I want you to know - actually *know* - the love of your Creator. Whether you're religious, spiritual, or entirely without faith in God, you'll see evidence in this book that serves as the foundation for confident faith in a loving God. More than anything else, you'll see and know that God is real, and that kind of confidence can and will change your life.

Almost everyone is on the fence. Most people just won't say it out loud.

"Religious" people like God because He makes them feel better.

"Spiritual" people like the idea of God, but they won't commit.

Skeptics like God, they just don't know Him yet or label His work appropriately.

And Christ-followers need more confidence in their God so they can live boldly.

With all of that said, this book is for three groups of people:

1. People who don't know God and are skeptical of God's existence

2. Religious or spiritual people who believe in God but lack confidence in their faith, and therefore they live like God doesn't exist

3. People who know God but simply want more confidence and boldness in their faith

The first two groups are what I would call hopeless. I know because I've been in both groups.

The first is unsure if there's a purpose to their existence, which is hopeless. You might be able to find a false sense of happiness through complacency and avoidance, but you won't find hope there.

The second has grown up religious, but now they're miserable because their life isn't going the way the Bible says it should. They're not sure *why* they believe, they doubt the God they claim to believe, and they're too afraid to admit it out loud. That's also hopeless.

For both of the first two groups of people, the skeptic and religious, all they know is here and now, and they simply wish for the best in the future. They're both living in equally hopeless scenarios and desperately need to know why they're on this Earth.

Regardless of which group you're currently in, if you're eager and open to finding truth, this book will be a breath of fresh air. If you're longing for a deep-rooted, securely grounded, and boldly confident faith, then the information in this book is for you.

My hope is that this book will open your eyes and lead you to experience life like you never have before. I firmly believe that this information will light a fire in your mind that digs deep down into your heart and changes who you are at your core for the better.

If you open your mind to the bigger picture that is painted throughout the pages of this book, I believe it will stir something inside of you that's been longing for fulfillment all your life. That's what this information has done for me, and I'm confident it will do the same for you.

Years of searching

I spent roughly 15 years searching for purpose and doubting God's existence. I grew up in church, but I never had a deep understanding of who God is. All of my years going to church and going through the motions as a child did very little for my faith, and by the time I hit my teenage years, I had all but given up on God.

Deep down, I thought God was too good to be true. The Bible sounded like a fairy tale, and frankly, when you grow up hearing the children's version of Bible stories, they can start to sound like fiction. And that's slowly how I started to see God.

I pictured God sitting on a throne somewhere in the clouds looking down on Earth with a huge staff in His hand. I'm not sure why, but in my mind, God looked like Ariel's dad in *The Little Mermaid*. You know, the big, old, bearded white guy. Now I can look back and laugh about it, but that shallow and uncertain view of God was leading me on a path towards overwhelming insecurity, fear, and hopelessness.

When I was in middle school, my older sister died suddenly in a car wreck at age 15, and my entire world was shaken. For the first time, I was forced to face the reality of death head-on, and it was terrifying. The blind faith I had been taught as a child was useless in that moment of harsh reality. When I desperately needed something real to cling to, all I had was a religion that had been handed down to me.

From then on, God became someone I only talked about when it was convenient and ignored the rest of the time. I started thinking that God was just a concept Christians clung to so that they didn't have to face the reality of the world around them, but I didn't ask many questions because I was too busy enjoying my life.

Then, at age 17, a close friend of mine died from an overdose on prescription drugs. Once again, just like five years prior, my world was shaken. And once again, my insecure beliefs led me further down a path of avoidance and hopelessness.

For the next eight years, I mostly avoided God, but I went to church from time to time when it made me feel better. That all changed when I got married, had a child, and was forced to grow up. Life's rough like that. You can't avoid the hard stuff forever. Eventually, you have to answer the hard questions.

***

When my wife and I had our first child, our son Jackson, I remember a few thoughts hit me almost immediately like a ton of bricks:

1. Life *really is* a miracle.

2. I don't know very much *at all* about how real-life works.

3. I need some serious help figuring this thing out.

4. And what in the world am I going to do when this kid grows up and asks me if God is real?

The last thought is the one that kept me up at night. Deep down, I had always been afraid to face that question for a couple of reasons: If I found that God wasn't real, life would be very depressing. On the other hand, if I found that God was real, that would be the end of all fun in my life. I'd have to move to Africa and dedicate myself to a life of khaki pants and Birkenstocks.

Either way, I knew I couldn't avoid it anymore. I had to figure out what I believed about God, and I had to make a decision fast. After all, I wasn't just responsible for my own eternal future anymore; I was responsible for the next generation's as well.

I knew that one day, my son would look to me for guidance. One day he would want to know why he's alive and what's going to happen to him when his life on Earth is over. I knew that eventually, he would face the same uncertainty that I had experienced, and I wanted him to be able to face it with confidence.

So, I dug in. For the next three years, I researched, read books, watched lectures, studied articles, took notes, and agonized over whether or not God was real. What I learned during that long period of intense research forever changed my life. At the end of it - after scrutinizing God from every angle I could find - I found myself giving in to the facts and trusting what had proven to be true.

In this book, I'll share with you what I learned over those several years of research. I'm not an expert, I'm just a writer and researcher who desperately needed hope and purpose, and I found them. This book is my way of simplifying it for you so you can find them, too.

Read on, and if you're bold enough to keep an open mind, you'll find that there truly is a strong foundation for belief in something much larger than your circumstances and faith that's grounded and cannot be shaken.

Section 1: What are you putting your faith in?

I want to start by making a claim that few people seem to understand: Regardless of whether or not you trust or believe in God, you *are* a person of faith. Faith is simply a synonym for trust. In that light, consider this:

- If you're inside a structure, you're trusting that the structure you're currently in will not collapse on you.

- If you're outside, you're trusting that the laws of gravity will not catapult you into space. (I suppose this also applies inside as well.)

- When you drive or ride in a vehicle, you're trusting that whoever built it tightened all the bolts, and whoever replaced the brakes last put everything back the right way.

- When you pass another vehicle on the road at high speeds, you're trusting that the driver of that vehicle will not suddenly turn ever-so-slightly in your direction.

- When you love someone, you're trusting that they will not break your heart.

We trust school curricula, news reports, our jobs, the stability of our economy, our government (if you didn't, you would move and stop paying taxes), and everything in-between. We trust that 9/11 actually happened, and the United States actually did land on the moon. Or some of us trust that it didn't happen. Either way, we're trusting a narrative from someone else.

Even if you have all the facts, there's always the possibility of being wrong. Life is a game of trust, and trust is just another word for faith. Some people have faith in science as an alternative to God. Other people have faith in apathy - that ignoring their uncertainty will all work out in the end.

So again, the most important question is, what are you putting your faith in? For some reason, we've come to believe that faith is a religious thing and that some people have it while others don't. But that's not the reality of the world we live in. We all have faith in something; it's just a matter of choosing where to place it.

What are you putting your faith in?

A vehicle has around 30,000 parts which all have to be put together by a human system that is subject to error, yet we put our faith in it every day without a second thought.

Certainty is an illusion. It doesn't exist. Faith is simply maintaining a belief in the absence of certainty. So, we all have faith. The only question is, what are you putting your faith in?

Given that scientists now know that they essentially know very little about the VAST majority of the universe, does it make sense to say with any certainty that there is no God?

To say that we have the answers after studying only a tiny fraction of a microscopic piece of the universe is a lot like:

- Walking into a forest,

- finding a single speck of dirt,

- examining it with a microscope until you learn everything you possibly can about it,

- then claiming to know everything about the forest, based on your extensive knowledge of your tiny speck of dirt.

There are many more amazing things in the vastness of the forest than can possibly be explained to someone who has only ever known a single speck of dirt.

And it's absolutely asinine for someone who only knows about a tiny speck of dirt to claim to know the answers to the most complex questions about the forest. No one would claim to have that kind of knowledge with such a tiny bit of information. Yet that's exactly what our society does.

If you're willing to go through life gambling on something so important with such little information, that's the worst example of the human ego destroying itself, and it's nothing short of a tragedy.

***

5 questions to ask yourself

The reason people don't believe in God has very little to do with facts and everything to do with their intellectual or emotional discomfort with uncertainty.

It's not that they know God *doesn't* exist, it's that they're just *uncertain* that He exists, and it really bothers them that they can't be more certain.

After all, there's no way to know for sure that God exists; therefore, it makes more sense to trust in what we can see and measure and know for certain, right?

The problem is, certainty is an illusion. It doesn't exist.

The thing many people - especially skeptical people - fail to realize is that they're typically not willing to address the uncertainty that comes with every aspect of human life, especially the field of science. Yet we put our faith in it.

Let's look at five of those uncertainties...

Certainty is an illusion.

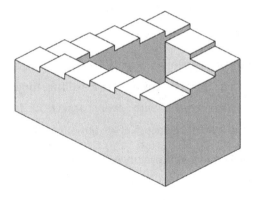

#1: Where did this all start?

Many people today point to the Big Bang as the origin of the universe, but for whatever reason, not many people seem to want to talk about what existed *before* that moment of creation.

Was it nothing? *Nothing* existed? That statement doesn't make sense. Was it a singularity that was infinitely small, hot, and dense? That makes even less sense. So, what was it?

Science tells us that all of the energy that exists in the universe today was created in an instant at the beginning of time, so whatever existed before the Big Bang must have been something outside of time, space, and our ability to comprehend. We have no way of grasping what must have existed before the Big Bang because this universe is *something*, and *something* doesn't come from *nothing*. That's cause and effect, and its common sense to us.

Scientists acknowledge the gap between the belief in a universe from nothing and the reality of cause and effect that surrounds us every day, and they've been trying to explain it without God for a long time. If you've spent any time reading theories developed by atheist and agnostic scientists about the beginning of time, you'll know that their theories can get downright bizarre.

How can anyone say that they can't believe in a God they don't see, yet they're willing to believe in theories that are based on things that no one has ever seen? Do you see the flaw in that?

Astrophysicist Hugh Ross[3] says it is because of this very conundrum – a universe from nothing with cause and effect –

that we now have scientific proof that God *does* exist. According to Ross, scientists now have space-time theorems that tell us space and time had a beginning and were created from something, implying that they must have something or *someone* beyond space and time that created our universe.[4]

The unavoidable truth is that what we see came from *somewhere*, even before the beginning of time itself. Let's move on to another question.

SOMETHING CAN'T COME FROM NOTHING.
– Cause and Effect

The chicken or the egg, one of them came first, but they did not come from nothing.

#2: Where did life come from?

Where did life come from? Evolution? But that's not the question. The question is, "Where did life *come from (originally)*?"

Modern science attempts to tell us how we became the humans we are today and how we've changed over time, and those are interesting theories, but they completely skip over the most important question, which is, "How did we get here in the first place?"

How is it that nonliving matter formed into living matter and then somehow survived and thrived without any help from *anyone*?

After all, there were no scientists there at the time to make sure the environment was controlled (unless you consider God the divine "scientist").

One article from Scientific America said, "The origin of life remains very much a mystery."[5] That article is *defending* evolution, yet they're forced to readily admit that they have no idea where life actually came from.

**Basically science:
The origin of life remains
very much a mystery.**

Based on current scientific theories, you might say:

"Maybe there are billions and billions and billions of universes where planets are forming and building blocks of life are being brought to those planets by comets hitting them, and then those planets are all harboring those chemicals until one of those planets finally has all the right ingredients to make life happen, and then it does. And here we are. It's not a miracle, then, just a long, long, long process."

But I would remind you, according to current scientific theories, you're only working with a total history of the universe of 13.8 billion years.[6] So, anyone who chooses to go with that theory must acknowledge the fact that the "billions and billions" of years is actually limited to 13.8 billion, according to scientific theories.

But let's go with that thought for a moment.

Let's look at a few of the "ingredients" that were necessary for this amazing process called life to successfully take place on our planet:

- It had to be the perfect distance away from the sun so that it didn't burn up or freeze.

- It had to have gravity to propel it in a perfect orbit around the sun to maintain that distance.

- It had to be made of rock.

- It had to be big enough to have a molten core so it could have a source of geothermal energy that wouldn't dissipate.

- It had to be able to have a protective atmosphere that holds carbon dioxide and other gases that keep the planet warm and protect its surface from radiation.

- Something (comets, asteroids?) had to bring water to its surface.

- Something (lightening, comets, asteroids?) had to bring the building blocks of life to its surface.

- Some kind of event had to happen to "spark" nonliving matter into living matter. There are several theories about how this could have happened, but it's still a mystery. Scientists are very uncertain.

- Once life was formed, nothing would have to extinguish it from existence.

According to astrophysicist Hugh Ross, the probability that you're going to find a body anywhere within this vast universe with the possibility of being able to sustain any kind of advanced life is more remote than someone in California winning the California lottery 150 consecutive times where they buy just one ticket each time.[7,8]

Common sense will tell you that we're in a pretty incredible predicament when it comes to things working for our advantage. Right now we're floating around in space being held at just the right distance from an incredibly dangerous heat source moving at exactly the right pace rotating at exactly the right speed with exactly the right amount of gravity to keep us stuck to the Earth which has exactly the right chemicals and environment for life to exist.

Not only is everything on our planet strangely and perfectly in place for life to exist, but all of life does exist and continues to exist despite countless reasons for it to be extinct.

Is it reasonable to believe that our life-friendly planet and the intelligent human beings that inhabit this planet all formed from gas and dust over just 13.8 billion years? Is it reasonable to believe that we, as complex human beings, are simply the product of chemical reactions? Yet somehow, the products of chemical reactions are able to understand how the chemical reactions happened?

In other words, that's like saying that we're the product of one giant science project, and now the science project knows that it's a science project, and it knows how the science project worked. Does that make any sense at all to you? That view goes against everything we are as humans.

What about intelligence, creativity, emotions, morality? Why do we all feel so destined for something more? Why does non-existence scare us so much?

Science is great. It's fascinating. But there's a serious issue when we look to a field of study for knowledge that can't begin to answer our most fundamental questions.

The truth is, science is filled with uncertainty.

Here's another one...

#3: How big is the universe?

This seems like a pretty basic question in the world of science, right?

The answer according to science (depending on who you ask): Approximately 93 billion light-years.

The problem is, that's just the observable universe - the part of the universe we can see from Earth - not the entire universe.

Imagine Earth is a ship sitting in the middle of an ocean. If we look out with binoculars in any direction, we can only see so far. Think of the distance we can see from the ship as our "observable ocean." That's similar to what the observable universe is. And that's what we're describing when we talk about how large the universe is.

We can only refer to the observable universe because that's all we can see from where we are. We know there's more out there - the universe doesn't just stop - but we don't know how much more is out there.

If you're the type of person who doesn't like uncertainty, that should bother you, especially if your faith is in knowledge.

THE REST OF
THE UNIVERSE

OBSERVABLE
UNIVERSE

EARTH

And even if scientists and astronomers do reach a point where they can narrow down the size of the entire universe, you could simply ask, "What's outside of that?"

And if they answer that, you could simply ask, "What's outside of that?"

That line of questioning could go on for a long time until science is forced to say, "I don't know."

Our brains think in terms of beginning and end. Everything we can see has something outside of it, something around it, something bigger than it. One thing stops, and another thing starts.

Houses, neighborhoods, cities, states, countries, continents, planets, galaxies, the universe...then what? Is the universe just infinitely large? Does it go on forever and ever?

When you start throwing out the idea of "infinity," you're getting into very uncertain territory and entering the territory of faith.

(Faith)

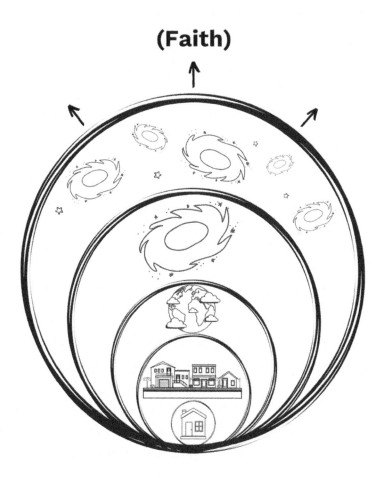

It's difficult for our minds to comprehend how large the entire universe is estimated to be. Think of it this way:

1 billion light-years = over 5,000,000,000,000,000,000,000 miles (that's over five sextillion miles).

45 billion light-years is about half the size of the *observable* universe, so that's about how far it would be to go from Earth to the end of the observable universe.

45 billion light-years = Over 264,000,000,000,000,000,000,000 miles (that's two hundred sixty-four sextillion miles)

To put that in perspective:

Earth is about 24,901 miles all the way around.

So, to travel from Earth to the end of the observable universe would be like traveling around the world over 10,000,000,000,000,000,000 times (that's 10 quintillion times).

Let's say it took you two days to fly around the world in an incredibly fast aircraft. Your journey to the end of the *observable* universe would take you more than 21,000,000,000,000,000,000 days (twenty-one quintillion days), and you would finish your journey somewhere near the year 58,000,000,000,000,000 (that's the year 57 quadrillion). Then you would still have to come back. And that's just the part of the universe we can see.

Now multiply that number times 3 with 23 zeros after it, and you have one estimate of how large the entire universe is. The answer, in miles, is roughly 7.9 with 46 zeros. Just writing that number would be hard, much less saying it. Yet that's the only way we have to communicate how large the universe is.

Regardless of how precise that number is, the point is this:

The universe we live in is larger than we can possibly comprehend, and we've only been able to catch a glimpse of a tiny, TINY fraction of a small piece of it.

Not to mention the fact that we've never actually explored beyond our own orbit, which, as we've covered, is not even a tiny speck on the map of the universe.

Odd, isn't it?

Our universe must be as close as we can comprehend to being infinite in size, yet scientists now believe that our universe had a beginning.

Those two concepts shouldn't be able to co-exist in our natural world, but they do. No matter which way you turn in science, you always end up with the unimaginable - the uncertain.

If that doesn't cast doubt on the scientific answer to the origin of the universe, you need to think about it a little longer.

and billions

Billions

and billions

Earth
↓
.

too many to count = faith

and quintillions

of miles

and sextillions

Then consider the next question...

#4: How small is the universe?

This question is fascinating to consider. Think about it for a second.

If I asked you, "What is the smallest unit of matter?" You would likely say an atom. If I asked you, "What are atoms made up of?" You would likely say protons, neutrons, and electrons.

If I asked you, "What are protons neutrons and electrons made up of?" You would likely say quarks and leptons. (Of course, because everyone knows what quarks and leptons are, right?)

But if I asked you what quarks and leptons are made up of, you would probably be forced to say you don't know. And scientists basically do the same thing, because our current microscopes can only see so far down into our microscopic universe.

And even if you could answer that question, I would just ask you, "What's that made up of?" And if you could answer that, I would ask again, "What's *that* made up of?" And that line of questioning could go on and on for a long time until you're finally forced to say, "I don't know."

As human beings, we can only see so far. Our microscopes don't have the resolution to make out something that small. In our minds, all matter is made up of other matter, so that's as far as our minds will take us. But the implication of that mindset is that all matter must have more matter inside of it.

Eventually, after we've looked in the microscope closer and closer and closer at the world around us, we simply call the smallest thing we can see "building blocks" because that's our way out of having to explain what those "building blocks" are made up of.

But eventually, all physical matter must have some sort of non-physical foundation. Either that or it's infinitely small, which is an idea we have no way of comprehending either. Infinity doesn't exist in the world we can see, and it doesn't make sense to our brains. It's unseen.

So, we're left with uncertainty.

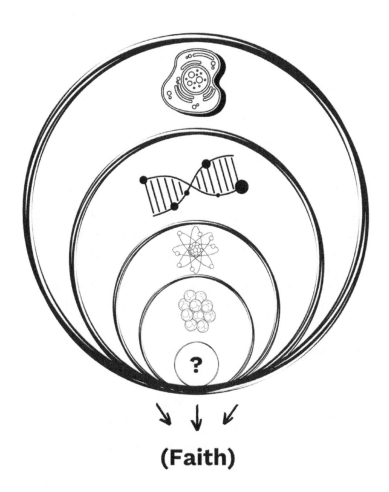

(Faith)

#5: What are dark matter and dark energy?

If you thought we knew anything at all about the universe, take a look at dark matter and dark energy. They will remind you just how little we actually know.

As it turns out, all of the physical matter we can see in the universe - planets, stars, gas, etc. - only make up about 4% of the universe.

The remaining 96% is dark matter and dark energy, and scientists don't know what they are.

They can't see dark matter and dark energy; they just know it's there based on their calculations. Other than that, dark matter and dark energy are basically mysteries to science, yet they make up the vast majority of our universe.

Space.com says, "All the stars, planets and galaxies that can be seen today make up just 4 percent of the universe. The other 96 percent is made of stuff astronomers can't see, detect, or even comprehend. These mysterious substances are called dark energy and dark matter."[9]

NASA says, "It turns out that roughly 68% of the universe is dark energy. Dark matter makes up about 27%. The rest - everything on Earth, everything ever observed with all of our instruments, all normal matter - adds up to less than 5% of the universe."[10]

NASA goes on to say, "Unfortunately, no one understands why the cosmological constant [dark energy] should even be there, much less why it would have exactly the right value to cause the observed acceleration of the universe."

That means in all our knowledge, all our centuries of studying the universe around us, we've only been looking at an almost embarrassingly small percentage of what's actually there.

In other words, the vast majority of "stuff" in the universe - even the parts of the universe we can see - is made up of something we can't see, measure, or understand.

That should make you second guess putting too much faith in science.

The most important question

Don't get caught up trying to use science to explain the origin of the universe and life. It just causes confusion. Science is great, but they can't tell us very much about the most important questions of our universe.

What you have to understand is that scientists don't have a crystal ball that allows them to look into the future (or the past, for that matter). They're simply observing the world around us and telling us what they think happened based on their observations.

That's what a theory is – it's a way of explaining something we don't or can't know with complete certainty. A theory is not an absolute fact. It's an idea based on what scientists know at that particular moment in time. It's not like scientists are out to fool everyone – the work they do is valuable and essential to the quality of life we all enjoy – but sometimes scientists get over-eager and exaggerate their findings to try to explain much more than they probably should.

If there's one thought that sums up scientific and human progress as a whole, it's this one: We're always certain about what we think we know until we don't know it anymore – *then* we're certain. In other words, we've always thought we had life figured out. That is until we learned something new. So, we must understand that flawed theories are normal.

For the origin of life on Earth, for example, last I checked, there are at least seven different theories on how it might have happened. And all of those theories come from well-meaning but limited people making educated guesses and giving possible scenarios.

Let me reiterate the point: Science is uncertain. Very uncertain. Considering how uncertain science is, it might be worth at least looking at the God of the Bible (which is the one book that claims to give us all the answers).

Because either way - science or God - you're going to be putting faith in something. You might as well know all your options before choosing.

So, the most important question is this: **What are you putting your faith in?**

Science, God, or anything else,
It's all faith.

So what's your faith in?

Section 2: Reasons to be Confident God Exists

Now that we've seen that faith exists wherever certainty is absent, and certainty is always absent, then it's time to go through some reasons you can believe with confidence that God is real and that He's with you.

After all, you're putting your future and your faith in something right now, so you might as well open your mind to something bigger than yourself – and this section will help you do so with confidence.

> **In the absence of any other proof, the thumb alone would convince me of God's existence.**
>
> **- ISAAC NEWTON**

Every beginning has a Beginner.

Scientists now believe that the universe had a beginning. That's a problem for people who deny there's a God.

Science tells us our universe is traceable back to a beginning, and several places (at least nine places) in the Bible speak about this beginning from nothing.[11]

The Bible is unique in that it actually speaks about the beginning of the universe as the beginning of space and time itself. Eastern faiths say space and time are eternal, and God creates within space and time, while Biblical faith says God is the Creator of space and time.

As we've covered already, space-time theorems tell us that any universe that expands on average has a space-time beginning, implying a Causal Agent outside space and time who creates space, time, matter, and energy.

In other words, there is now scientific knowledge that essentially proves that there was a cosmic beginning, which implies a "Someone" beyond space and time, which must have created the universe.

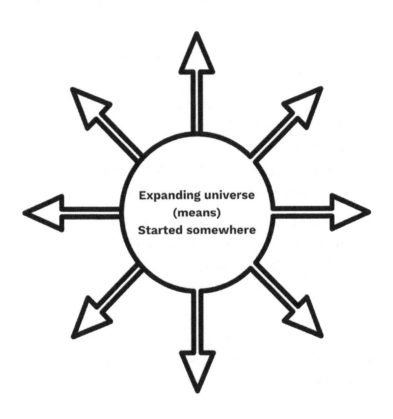

Expanding universe
(means)
Started somewhere

There are more than a few scientific facts regarding the beginning of the universe that point to the reality of God.

Frank Turek[12], author of the book *I Don't Have Enough Faith to Be an Atheist*, lists a few of the main ones using the acronym SURGE:

- Second law of thermodynamics

- Universe is expanding

- Radiation afterglow

- Great galaxy seeds

- Einstein's general relativity

Each one of these five pieces of scientific evidence all supports the idea that the universe had a beginning. With evidence now pointing to our universe having a beginning, we're running out of reasons to avoid the One who started it.

Robert Jastrow, who founded NASA's Goddard Institute of Space Studies and is a self-proclaimed agnostic, said that "the astronomical evidence leads to a Biblical view of the origin of the world."[13]

He also said that the essential elements in the astronomical and biblical accounts of Genesis are the same.[14] And this is coming from a world-renown agnostic astronomer.

But let's think about the alternative. Why couldn't nature have started itself?

We covered this briefly already, but everything we see functions on the principle of cause and effect. Nature is the effect; therefore, it cannot also be the cause. Before the universe existed, there was no nature - no space, time, or matter. There was nothing.

So, one of these two must be true:

> Either NO ONE created something out of nothing

> or

> SOMEONE created something out of nothing.

There is no third option; it really is that simple. So, which is more reasonable?

ART ISN'T ACCIDENTAL.

Where there is design, there must be a Designer.

Aspects of the universe - such as the laws of nature - are so fine-tuned that if you were to change any one of these aspects even slightly, there would be no life here on Earth.

Stephen Hawking said if the expansion rate of the universe were different by one part in a hundred thousand million million a second after the Big Bang, the universe would have collapsed back on itself or never developed galaxies.[15]

Our current expansion rate - sometimes called the cosmological constant - is fine-tuned to 1 in 10 to the 20 (1 with 20 zeros). The gravitational force is fine-tuned to 1 in 10 to the 40 (1 with 40 zeros). If it were altered, the sun wouldn't be here, and neither would we.

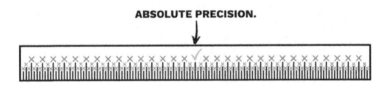

Imagine taking a tape measure and stretching it across the entire known universe, then setting the gravitational force at a particular inch mark on that tape measure. If you were to move the strength of gravity one inch in either direction, we wouldn't be here. There are only three possible explanations for this extreme precision:

1. **It happened out of necessity.** This is farfetched at best. Any of these fine-tuned aspects of the universe could have been different by a little or by a whole lot.

2. **It happened by chance.** I don't have enough faith to believe that it just happened to arrive there by chance. And by the way, "chance" isn't a cause or force in nature. Chance is just a word that scientists use to explain mathematical possibilities. What they really mean is that they don't know.

3. **Somebody designed it.**

Our solar system also seems to be fine-tuned with us in mind:

- If our planet were a little closer, we would burn up. If we were a little further away, we would freeze. It's just right where we're at.

- If the axial tilt changes just a little, we wouldn't exist.

- If the rotation of the earth changes, we wouldn't exist.

- If the size and distance of the moon were different, we wouldn't exist.

- If the amount of oxygen in the atmosphere (21%) were any different, we wouldn't exist. 15% and we all suffocate. 25% and spontaneous fires break out.

- If Jupiter were not in its current orbit, we wouldn't be here. Its gravitational force is so strong, it attracts meteors and other space junk to it and away from Earth. In fact, Jupiter has comet fragment strikes that are bigger than the Earth. Thank God for Jupiter.

- The average distance between stars in our galaxy is 30 trillion miles. That distance is needed for the Earth to exist in its current life-supporting condition. If it were much different, gravitational forces would cause us to not stay in orbit, and we wouldn't be able to live.

If you traveled the speed of a space shuttle - roughly 5 miles per second - it would take you about 200,000 years to get from the sun (our star) to the nearest star in our galaxy. There are approximately as many grains of sand on all the beaches of the earth as there are stars in the universe, and going from one star to another star would take about 200,000 years. That should give you a picture of how large our universe is, yet without this expansive universe of ours, without its mass being just right, life as we know it wouldn't be possible.

Psalm 19:1 says, "The heavens are telling of the glory of God; And their expanse is declaring the work of His hands." Look to the heavens, and you'll have an idea of an infinite being.

Our universe is the perfect size. If it were any bigger or smaller, we wouldn't exist.

You can also see evidence of God in a microscope when looking at a "simple" form of life.

A cell is like a factory, and in these factories, there are very detailed and specific messages being used to make certain things. We know that messages only come from intelligent beings.

For example, if you walked in your kitchen and on your table, there laid a knocked-over box of alpha-bits cereal, and the letters spelled, "Take out the trash – Mom," you wouldn't assume that the box fell over on its own and spelled that.

There are only four known forces of nature: gravity, electromagnetism, strong nuclear force, and weak nuclear force. The laws of nature describe the things these four forces do repetitively, but they can't explain a message in the cell.

These messages are called DNA, which is the 4-letter genetic alphabet that every living thing has. But where does it come from?

Your genome is 3.5 billion letters long, and all the letters are in just the right order, or you wouldn't be here.

There's no known chemical, physical, or biological force that can explain why the letters up the spine of the DNA molecule are in the order they're in. A goes with T, and C goes with G, but there's no reason or force that can explain the order in which they go.

DNA is literally a program, and whenever there's a program, there must be a Programmer.

DNA is a program. Programs don't evolve.

For the sake of conversation, let's say life started simply, like in an amoeba.

The problem with that theory is that programs don't evolve. If anything, they deteriorate over time.

If you took any program and randomly mutated the code over time, it wouldn't work very long. Even when left alone, programs don't fare well. Just try not updating your iPhone for a few years and see how well it works.

Richard Dawkins - one of the most famous atheists in the world - said that in one amoeba, a single-celled organism, there's the equivalent of 1,000 volumes of an encyclopedia.[16]

And you could fit several hundred amoebas in one inch.

To believe that resulted from natural forces is like believing the Library of Congress resulted from an explosion in a printing shop.

I don't have enough faith to believe that.

Human DNA is like a computer program but far, far more advanced than any software ever created.

- BILL GATES

There are over 1,000 Encyclopedias worth of information in a single-celled organism.

DNA

According to Dr. Frank Turek, when you were conceived, you beat approximately 300 million other sperm in order to be born.[17] Your "soldier" was 20-30x smaller than a grain of salt, yet it contained half of the genetic information that makes you who you are.

Your mother's egg was about the size of a period at the end of a sentence in an average book, and it contained the other half of the genetic information that makes you who you are.

And when those two came together, a 100% new genetic human being was created.

You have not received any more genetic information from that point until right now. Time, air, water, and food were the only things that separated you from adulthood at that moment.

Genetically you were the same as a two-year-old or a full-grown adult.

From that moment until now, an astonishing construction project has been taking place. According to Dr. Turek, from the moment of your conception, cells began multiplying at an astonishing rate. Some became heart cells, some lung cells, some brain cells.

How do they know how to do this? *We don't know.*

Right now, your body makes 2 million red blood cells per second, and you do it without ever thinking about it. Aristotle calls this final causality, which points out that the entire created order is goal-directed. It's going in a direction.

Why is an embryo goal-directed to become an adult? Why does an acorn always become an oak tree instead of something else? Because they're goal-directed to become those things.

Why do the planets circle the sun? Why is gravity consistently doing what it's doing? Because it's goal-directed.

Why can we build a rover and launch it to another planet 60 million miles away with absolute precision? Because we can depend on the forces of nature being consistent and precise because they're goal-directed.

In order to be goal-directed, there must be an external Intellect directing them. Somebody is holding the universe together right now, directing it toward an end - both living and nonliving.

Here's what I mean...

Scientists have manipulated fruit fly embryos to see what will happen to them, but the embryo makes heroic efforts to get back on track to becoming a fruit fly.[18]

When scientists do this, they always get one of 3 outcomes:

1. A normal fruit fly

2. A mutant fruit fly

3. A dead fruit fly

FRUIT FLY   (OUR BEST EFFORTS)   STILL A
                                           FRUIT FLY

They never get a different type of fly, much less anything else beyond that. Yet we have theories in science now that claim these species can blur the lines between one another over long periods of time, and when we try with all our intelligence to blur these lines to go from one species to another, we can't. But we're led to believe that non-intelligent processes can do it?

No matter what you believe about evolution, there must be an external intellect holding together the natural forces of nature that allow all life to occur. Even if you hold to the belief that macroevolution is true, you still can't get rid of the need for an external intellect, i.e., God.

DNA is just one more reminder that everything in the universe is moving forward with information and purpose.

Darwinians believe life *looks* as though it was designed; they just refuse to believe that it was. Instead, they say it has been guided by natural selection and random mutations. Darwin thought that nature could do the selecting and guiding of adaptations instead of God. In his opinion, it's *nature* just doing what *nature* does.

[Side note: What's very interesting is that the term "nature" is simply a label for a collection of observable truths around us. Replace the word "nature" with the name "God" and you have the exact same facts, just crediting God. It doesn't change the truth. Back to DNA...]

When Darwin developed his theory, it was thought that the cell was simple. But now we know that the cell has immense informational complexity.

Inside DNA, we've discovered a 4-character digital code that Bill Gates says is like a computer program that's far, far more advanced than any we've ever created. We now know that the information in DNA directs the construction of other complicated molecules called proteins, which do all the important functional jobs in the cell, including the construction of machines.

Proteins are made up of subunits called amino acids. There are 20 different kinds of these, and the arrangement of these 20 different kinds of amino acids determines the shape the protein will form. The shape of the protein determines its function, so the arrangement of the amino acids has to be correct for the protein to accomplish its job inside the cell.

How does all this happen? Instructions on the DNA molecule are directing the production of those proteins, and it's incredibly complex. The average protein is about 300 amino acids in length. Some have thousands of amino acids, all linked together with precision.

This information has to be formed exactly right, or it won't form with the right shape, and the protein won't do its job. And it's the information on DNA that gets it exactly right.

So, DNA directs the arrangement of amino acids in just the right way to form just the right proteins that do just the right jobs.

cgcggtagaatcgtttgttgtcggctgtgtcgcctccttgtgaggaactaccgcacgata
cttatatgtcccctagtctcaaacgggctcaattctgacggttccatcgcgaagatctac
tcctaccgacggtccacccgcagtcaacatggtcacggtgaatgtgagaaacgccctatg
ccgtctacggccacttgctgtgcgataagtccgtggaacacggaatgcttccttatagtc...

This "code" makes you YOU.

J. Warner Wallace, in his book *Cold Case Christianity*, puts it this way:

"The building blocks of life (proteins, ribosomes, enzymes, etc.) are formed at the direction of specific nucleotide sequencing in DNA, the largest molecule known. In humans, DNA contains as many as 10 billion atoms. The adenine, guanine, cytosine, and thymine bases in DNA are linked in a particular order to form the genetic code containing the master plan for every organism. The information in DNA guides and instructs the formation of proteins; without it, protein formation would be a haphazard, hit-or-miss proposal. The nucleic sequence in DNA is informational."

Inside every cell in you is a three-billion-letter DNA structure that belongs only to you. 99.9% of your DNA is similar to everyone's genetic makeup. What makes you unique is the fractional difference in how those three billion letters are sequenced in your cells.

Dr. Francis Collins, director of the Human Genome Project (that mapped the human DNA structure), said that one can "think of DNA as an instructional script, a software program, sitting in the nucleus of the cell."[19]

He also said:

"It is humbling for me and awe-inspiring to realize that we have caught the first glimpse of our own instruction book, previously known only to God."[20]

Miniature Machines

More evidence for God can be found in the miniature machines inside cells.[21]

The cell is the smallest unit of life. Yet even in single-celled organisms like bacteria, we find exquisite machinery.

Dr. Stephen Meyer, who received his Ph.D. in the philosophy of science from the University of Cambridge and now directs Discovery Institute's Center for Science and Culture, says this about one of these cellular machines:

"[A bacterial flagellum motor] is a rotary engine, and it turns at 100,000 RPM in some bacterial species. It has a rotor, a stator, a u-joint, a propeller-like tail that allows the bacterium to propel itself through liquid; it's hardwired into a signal transduction circuit which allows the bacterium to change directions on a quarter-turn of the rotary engine to chase down the food supply. It's an extraordinary piece of high technology in low life."

Meyer says that systems like this are very difficult to explain by Darwinian evolution. Natural selection is a mechanism that selects for functional advantage. Therefore, variations that offer advantages are passed on to the next generation.

The problem is, the origin of systems like this can't be explained by natural selection, because these systems have no functional advantage until many different independent parts are all brought into close functional integration.

For example, according to Meyer, a bacterial flagellum motor is made of roughly 30 protein parts. If you knock out one of those protein parts, you disable a gene for building one of those parts, and the "one-part-less" version of that motor doesn't work. It doesn't provide propulsion or a functional advantage.

If you're trying to build up a motor like this gradually in Darwinian fashion, there are big gaps where there's no functional advantage in getting from point A to B.

This is not the kind of system that can be explained by natural selection. It's an appearance of design - it's a rotary engine - and it cannot be adequately explained by gradual natural selection and random variation.

Michael Behe, Professor of Biological Sciences at Lehigh University in Pennsylvania and a Senior Fellow at Discovery Institute's Center for Science and Culture, calls molecular machinery like this an example of "irreducible complexity."

Whenever we see this irreducible complexity and trace it back to its source, we always come to a mind or intelligence. And there are dozens of these types of molecular machines inside of biology and inside living cells. A few examples include:

- Sliding clamps
- Information recognition devices that control the flow of information in and out of the cell nucleus
- Turbines called "ATP synthases" that are responsible for generating the information that cells use in the process of metabolism

These all require the integration of many separate parts and are therefore very difficult to explain by Darwinian evolution.

In his book *Darwin's Black Box*, Dr. Behe says, "Biochemistry has, in fact, revealed a molecular world that stoutly resists explanation by the same theory so long applied at the level of the whole organism."[22]

Darwin never imagined the exquisitely profound complexity that exists even at the most basic levels of life.

- PROFESSOR MICHAEL BEHE, PHD

If there's anything morally wrong, there must be a God who sets the moral standard.

If there is no God, then the Holocaust was just a difference of opinion - the world's opinion versus Hitler's opinion. But we know that's not right. We know the Holocaust was objectively morally wrong.

If you saw two versions of a map of Scotland, how would you know which one was correct or which one was better? You would have to have a real, unchanging map of Scotland to compare each of them to. If we compare Mother Teresa to Hitler, how do we know which one was better? We have to compare each of them to an ultimate, unchanging standard. That standard is God.

My argument against God was that the universe seemed so cruel and unjust. But how had I got this idea of just and unjust? A man does not call a line crooked unless he has some idea of a straight line.

- C.S. LEWIS

If there is no God:

1. The Nazis were not wrong.

2. Love is no better than rape.

3. There are no human rights.

4. Tolerance is no better than intolerance.

5. Religious crusades are not wrong.

6. We can't complain about the problem of evil because evil can't exist unless you have some idea of what good is. You can't know a line is crooked without having a straight line to compare it to.

In other words, the shadows prove the sunshine. You can have sunshine (good) without shadows (evil), but you can't have shadows without sunshine.

Undeniable

When you look around at the universe we live in and the complexity of life on Earth, it's very difficult to come up with an alternate logical explanation. In fact, in an interview with Ben Stein, well-known atheist Richard Dawkins said that even he believes in intelligent design.[23]

His exact words were:

> *"It could be that at some earlier time somewhere in the universe a civilization evolved by probably some kind of Darwinian means to a very very high level of technology and designed a form of life that they seeded onto perhaps this planet. Now that is a possibility, and an intriguing*

possibility, and I suppose it's possible that you might find evidence for that if you look at the details of biochemistry, molecular biology, you might find a signature of some sort of designer. And that designer could well be a higher intelligence from elsewhere in the universe."

Then he says:

"That higher intelligence would itself have had to have come about by some explicable, or ultimately explicable process. It couldn't have just jumped into existence spontaneously, that's the point."

Apparently, at least in Richard Dawkins' mind, the evidence is so strong for intelligent design that he has to come up with a random and unsupported theory of aliens bringing life to Earth. And even that theory just puts the question back one step. The next question would be, who created the aliens? Like Dawkins said, "it (life) couldn't have just jumped into existence spontaneously." Of course not. Not without a Creator.

As Ben Stein said, Richard Dawkins isn't against a designer, just certain designers, such as God.

Why is Dawkins against the idea of an intelligent God but not intelligent aliens? Because God brings morality and accountability with Him, and aliens don't.

Dawkins also says that God is "hidden," or hiding Himself, but that's just another example of worldview changing the way we see the evidence. What more could God do to reveal Himself?

He came to Earth in human form (Jesus Christ) and did miraculous things to prove that He is who He says He is. Then we killed him. (We'll cover that later on in the book.)

He's given us intelligence to understand this amazing universe we live in.

He's given us the ability to study DNA and molecular machines and all kinds of other amazingly complex things to show us just how orchestrated life is.

He's given us morality, emotions, imagination, and creativity to set us apart from other animals and to show us that we're different - and we can't explain where these things came from.

He's given us love, which by itself should show us that life is much bigger than what we see in front of us.

But instead of taking all of this evidence as evidence for God, some people would rather come up with unsupported theories to try to explain it away.

It's not a matter of evidence. It's a matter of stubbornness. It's a matter of pride.

Evidence for God is everywhere:

- The beginning of the universe

- The fine-tuning of nature

- Life itself

- DNA

- Morality

- Creativity

- Intelligence

- Emotions

- Jesus Christ doing miracles and rising from the dead

- And more

Skeptics like Richard Dawkins simply fail to accept it for what it is – overwhelming evidence of a designed universe.

The
Bible
is
the
only
ancient
book
that
told
us
about
our
universe
before
we
saw
it
for
ourselves.

The laws of physics point to something much bigger.

You may not think about this very often, but the world around us is extremely consistent. Think about it: We live in a universe that is so dependable we can actually predict when the sun will rise and set every single day of the year. The timing changes ever-so-slightly each day, yet we can predict that timing with precision because the universe is so incredibly consistent.

Over the course of history, scientists have observed this consistency in nature and recorded what they've found in the form of laws. These laws of nature, or laws of physics, describe what scientists repeatedly see without fail in the universe.

The Bible says that the more we study nature, the more evidence we will uncover for the handiwork and the attributes of God (see Job, Psalms, and Romans). So, what do the laws of nature tell us about God?

First, the Bible tells us to look at the laws that govern the heavens and the Earth, because as they *don't change*, God *doesn't change*. In other words, the more we study the laws of physics, the more we see just how much they point back to the unchanging God described in the Bible.

Virtually every feature of the laws of physics reveals overwhelming evidence for fine-tuning design. According to Hugh Ross, starting in 1991, there were 17 features of the universe and laws of physics that showed a high level of fine-tuning design, but now there are over 200 features that we know must be fine-tuned.[24] The more we learn, the more evidence we see for God's handiwork and attributes.

Not only do these discoveries point us to a Designer, but astronomers and physicists also can't help but notice that when you look at the universe and the laws that govern it, it's clear that it was designed for the specific *benefit* of human beings. It's also clear that the Creator intended to redeem billions of human beings. Here's what I mean...

Of all the laws of physics, the Bible focuses mostly on the law of decay.

It says in Romans, chapter 8, that the entire creation is subject to the law of decay. It says the whole creation "groans" and that creation itself will one day be liberated from its bondage to decay and brought into the freedom and glory of the children of God. But what is it about the law of decay that helps bring about the freedom and glory of the children of God?

Here's the cool thing: According to Dr. Hugh Ross, we actually live in a universe that has the optimal physics for the defeat and removal of evil and for willing human beings to receive redemption. That applies to every law of physics and every dimension of space and time. It's all been designed to bring about the removal of evil and suffering and the redemption of billions of human beings.

When it comes to the law of decay, Ross says the decay rate is not so high as to discourage productive work and not so low as to let evil go unrestrained. If we could do something and have it last forever with no decay, there would be no restraint against human evil.

In Genesis, chapter 3, when Adam and Eve sinned, God said they would experience more pain, work, and wasted time.

God made the law of decay so neither our work nor our bodies would last forever, serving as a constant reminder that we need God's help. Without His help, life is nothing but pain, work, and wasted time.

God intended that work and the sense of touch would be pleasurable. But because of human sin and evil, we now experience more pain, more work, and more wasted time.

Sin leads to more pain, work, and wasted time, and because we all despise these things, they act as powerful motivation for us to avoid evil, and it teaches us that we can't avoid these things (and sin) without help.

If we look at the universe, we realize that God is all-powerful and all-loving, and we can't deliver ourselves from the consequences of our sin and evil. But because of God's power and love, He provided a way out.

The mass of the universe is exactly right.

According to Ross, we need exactly 50 billion trillion stars for life to be possible. He says we wouldn't be able to get carbon and oxygen unless the universe has a highly fine-tuned total mass.[25] So, the fact that the universe is massive doesn't make us insignificant. As it turns out, it's all necessary for us to live.

The human body is incredible.

We covered DNA, but the rest of the human body is also amazingly complex. For example, a team of neuroscientists from MIT found that the human brain can process entire images that the eye sees for as little as 13 milliseconds.[26]

And consider the human eye, which works like a camera. Similar to the shutter of a camera, the iris and the pupil control how much light to let into the back of the eye. When it's dark, our pupils get larger to let in more light. And just like the lens of a camera is able to focus on objects using mirrors and other mechanical devices, the lens of our eye helps us focus in coordination with other parts of the eye. It's all working together in an incredibly intricate and complex way.[27]

In fact, everything in our bodies seems to exist for a purpose, and each part works together to keep us alive. The question is, how did our bodies get this complex and perfectly put together?

Consciousness and intelligence are mind-boggling to even think about.

This one's kind of deep, but stick with me. Have you stopped to consider where consciousness and awareness of ourselves and our surroundings come from?

If we truly are nothing more than the product of a fortunate series of chemical reactions, isn't it odd that we're now aware and intelligent enough to be able to understand how it all works? That seems more than a bit unlikely to me.

The more reasonable conclusion is that consciousness and mental capacity for reasoning must come from an external force capable of such things.

HUMAN EYE

THE HUMAN BRAIN CAN PROCESS
ENTIRE IMAGES THAT THE EYE SEES
IN AS LITTLE AS 13 MILLISECONDS.

Where do emotions come from?

Where do emotions come from? In many ways, they get in the way of evolution. Jealousy, anger, envy - these all do more harm than good most of the time.

Anger can be used for survival, but it's far from necessary. It actually clouds your judgment and causes you to make mistakes more often than not.

Love causes people to make stupid decisions. You can have sexual desire (lust) without love, so what evolutionary purpose does love serve?

Why do we love people even when they turn their backs on us? If love is just a product of evolution that only serves to further our species, it's doing a terrible job of it.

In loving and serving, we prove that we have been created in the likeness of God

- MOTHER TERESA

Disgust (an emotion) makes almost everyone dislike food that is good for them and enjoy food that will actually kill them over time. Why is that? That should be the exact opposite in an evolutionary worldview. If healthy food makes us thrive, why do we hate it so much after all these years?

Why are we so creative?

Why are we so creative? Where does imagination come from? Did it evolve somehow, too?

Where do art and music come from? They serve no purpose at all from an evolutionary or naturalistic standpoint.

All of these points together build a cumulative case for a Creator.

Section 3: Reasons to Trust the Bible

Throughout history, human beings, both individually and entire cultures, have based their knowledge of life on the words in the Bible.

The Bible gives details regarding the universe, the stars, our planet, the water cycle, and much, much more - things no one could have possibly known thousands of years ago when the Bible was written. But for the first time in history, human beings have now gathered enough information from the natural world around them to feel like they're able to actually challenge the Bible's wisdom.

However, before we start challenging the wisest book in human history, we have to truly understand that for thousands of years, the Bible was THE source of knowledge for many people, and they did very well with that knowledge.

What's exceptional is, even today, with all the technology and research tools at our disposal, the Bible is still completely accurate. With the wealth of knowledge available in the modern world, the question we're faced with is, "Is the Bible trustworthy?"

All things most desirable for man's welfare, here and hereafter, are to be found portrayed in it [the Bible].

- ABRAHAM LINCOLN

A thorough knowledge of the Bible is worth more than a college education.

- THEODORE ROOSEVELT

Within the covers of the Bible are the answers for all the problems men face.

- RONALD REAGAN

The Bible is strangely consistent.

The Bible is made up of 66 books written over more than 1,500 years by 40 different authors in all different locations and from every walk of life. It was written in palaces, prisons, and every setting in-between. It was written by shepherds, fishermen, physicians, tax collectors, tent makers, kings, prophets, and others. Yet they all tell different parts of the same story with amazing consistency.

Throughout history, human beings have proven to be quite good at messing things up, so if the Bible is only the work of human beings, it would have to be the most intricate and amazing piece of written work ever completed. In other words, if you can make yourself believe that the Bible is simply the work of humans, you're putting a TON of faith in the ability of human beings to not mess things up.

The Bible was written...

IN 66 BOOKS

BY 40 WRITERS

**ACROSS
3 CONTINENTS**

**OVER MORE THAN
1,500 YEARS**

And it tells one remarkably consistent story.

If you can make yourself believe the Bible is simply the work of humans, you're putting a ton of faith in the ability of human beings to not make mistakes.

(See RMS Titanic, 1912)

When it comes to the Bible, it wasn't as if one person wrote a part of the story and then handed it off to another person to pick it up from there. Instead, the Bible is filled with writings from people who had no relation or known connection to one another. It even has some overlapping moments where multiple writers were likely writing close to the same time in history but in completely different locations and with no knowledge of the other person's writing.

Imagine if you wrote a book, then your great-great grandchild's neighborhood friend wrote a book, then someone who lived at the same time as their great-great-great grandchild but lived on the other side of the state and never met them wrote a book, then that person's great-great-great-great grandchild's distant neighbor's acquaintance from a different country altogether wrote a book, and so on and so forth over the course of more than 1,500 years.

Then, thousands of years later, people look back at all the books you and they wrote and see that they all tell different parts of the same exact story. They all have the same hero, and they all describe this hero in the exact same way from different points of view.

You would think that eventually, someone's imagination would start to wander, and they'd end up with a slightly different story than the others before them. But not in these stories. Instead, they all tell different parts of one consistent story. That's amazing to think about.

The Koran was written by Mohammed. The Analects of Confucius were written by Confucius. The writings of Buddha were written by Buddha. It makes sense that these would follow a consistent theme.

But the Bible stands alone as a group of books written by different authors at different times in history and in different places, all unified by one central theme and all describing God as the exact same person, but in different ways.

And all of this goes without mentioning the amount of influence and impact the Bible has had on both individuals and societies. It would be no exaggeration to say that the Bible is easily the most influential book of all time, and it has radically changed countless lives over the thousands of years it's been around.

The Bible predicted Jesus' life.

Many ancient Old Testament books in the Bible predicted almost every aspect of Jesus' life hundreds of years before it happened.

Some might be tempted to say that the writers of the New Testament knew about the prophecies in the Old Testament regarding the Messiah, so they made up or exaggerated stories about Jesus in order to make it line up better with the prophecies. This, some might say, is a confirmation bias in action.

The problem with that is, we have secular (non-Christian) historical evidence that tells us the following:

- Jesus actually existed in the time He was said to have existed

- Jesus lived in Judea

- His followers believed He did miraculous things

- Jesus was rejected by His own people (the Jews)

- Jesus died due to crucifixion

- His disciples believed they had experienced the risen Jesus

- His disciples' lives were transformed, and they spent their lives telling people about Him

Those are the things we know about Jesus based on *non-Christian* sources, and they only confirm what the Bible says about Jesus.

"...independent historical sources [non-Christian and Jewish] confirm what we are told in the Gospels

- DR. LAWRENCE MYKYTIUK

Extra-biblical sources confirm what we read in the gospels

- DR. WILLIAM LANE CRAIG

What did the Old Testament say hundreds of years before about these things that we know happened to Jesus?

Check this out:

Prediction	When it was predicted	When it happened
The Messiah will come at a specific time	Daniel 9:25-26	Galatians 4:4 and Ephesians 1:10
The Messiah will be born in Bethlehem (which is in Judea)	Micah 5:2	Matthew 2:1 and Luke 2:4-7
Messiah would be rejected by his own people.	Psalm 69:8 Isaiah 53:3	John 1:11 John 7:5
Messiah would be crucified with criminals.	Isaiah 53:12	Matthew 27:38 Mark 15:27-28
Messiah would resurrect from the dead.	Psalm 16:10 Psalm 49:15	Matthew 28:2-7 Acts 2:22-32

All of the books in the "When it was predicted" column above are books that were written hundreds of years before the ones under the "When it happened" column.

In other words, all 5 of the predictions above were written down hundreds of years before they came true, and we have documented non-Christian sources that confirm that all of these are historical facts.

The question is, how could the Old Testament writers have predicted these facts if the Bible isn't what it claims to be – written word of God?

Jesus fulfilled hundreds of prophecies from the Old Testament of the Bible, and the probability of anyone fulfilling even a small number of Old Testament prophecies is mind-bogglingly improbable.

Peter Stoner, Chairman of the Departments of Mathematics and Astronomy at Pasadena City College until 1953, says in his book *Science Speaks*[28] that the chance of Jesus accidentally fulfilling just 8 prophecies from the Old Testament is 1 in 10^{17} (that's 1 with 17 zeros after it).

Here's how he illustrates that probability:

"Suppose that we take 10^{17} silver dollars and lay them on the face of Texas. They will cover all of the state two feet deep. Now mark one of these silver dollars and stir the whole mass thoroughly, all over the state. Blindfold a man and tell him that he can travel as far as he wishes, but he must pick up one silver dollar and say that this is the right one. What chance would he have of getting the right one? Just the same chance that the prophets would have had of writing these eight prophecies and having them all come true in any one man, from their day to the present time, providing they wrote using their own wisdom.

Now these prophecies were either given by inspiration of God or the prophets just wrote them as they thought they should be. In such a case the prophets had just one chance in 10^{17} of having them come true in any man, but they all came true in Christ."

Stoner then adds that most people are very comfortable taking much riskier odds on business deals. In fact, a 9 out of 10 chance of success is usually seen as a worthwhile investment in almost any area of our lives. That's only a 1 in 10 chance that it won't work out. Those are odds that most anyone would take.

If that's the case, then why are we so reluctant to trust something that is exponentially less likely to be false than 1 out of 10?

To simplify it, there's a 99.999999999999999% chance that Jesus was who He said He was – the one who was predicted to have been sent by God to save mankind. Jesus is the surest bet you'll ever make, yet for some reason, some still find it hard to trust Him.

Science lines up with the Bible (not the other way around).

I find it interesting how many people see a dichotomy of worldviews in their minds. On one side, they see a worldview that is based on science, and on the other side, they see a worldview that is based on the Bible. For some reason, they think they have to choose between the two.

We often end up in this "one or the other" mindset, and since science is well represented in school curricula from a very young age and the Bible is not at all, we often end up "siding" with science.

But that dichotomy is unnecessary and imaginary. Science and the Bible are not on opposing sides. Scientists experience things and write them down. Ancient Biblical writers experienced things and wrote them down. Both are evaluating the same reality, yet we disregard whichever one challenges our comfort zone.

But one thing I find particularly fascinating is the fact that science and the Bible line up very well in regard to their observations of how the universe was made.

Hugh Ross is one of the best resources for this conversation about the Biblical narrative compared to the scientific one.

Dr. Ross is an astronomer and best-selling author of books such as *Improbable Planet, Navigating Genesis, Hidden Treasures in the Book of Job*, and *Why the Universe Is the Way It Is*. He has a degree in physics from the University of British Columbia, a National Research Council of Canada fellowship, and a Ph.D. in astronomy from the University of Toronto. In 2012, Hugh, together with Dr. Gerald Schroeder, received the Ide P. Trotter Prize presented by Texas A&M University in recognition of his work in demonstrating connections between science and religion. He has also spoken at hundreds of universities and churches, as well as numerous conferences around the world.

In other words, he's very knowledgeable and credible to speak in this area.

Here's what Dr. Ross says about how science lines up with the Bible[29]...

The creation and expansion of the physical universe

Genesis chapter one says that God created the "heavens and the earth."

In the Old Testament Hebrew, there is no word for "universe." Instead, they used the phrase "heavens and earth," which referred to all physical matter, energy, space, and time.

According to Ross, space-time theorems say that if the universe contains mass (which it does) and if general relativity reliably describes the movements of bodies in the universe (and it does), then the universe had a beginning which includes the beginning of space and time itself.

Prominent atheist Stephen Hawking wrote that "the universe has not existed forever. Rather, the universe, and time itself, had a beginning."[30]

As it turns out, the scientific community not only proved that time was created, but they also proved that the Bible, of all the religious books in the world, got it right.

Non-biblical religions tell us that God or gods or cosmic forces create within space and time, and space and time eternally exist. But the Bible stands alone in saying that space and time did not exist until God created the universe.

Now we have scientific theorems that actually prove this is correct.

Lawrence Krauss, one of America's most famous atheists, wrote in his book *Universe from Nothing*, "The apparent logical necessity of First Cause is a real issue for any universe that has a beginning. Therefore, on the basis of logic alone one cannot rule out such a deistic view of nature."[31]

Skeptics the world over have wrestled with this. They know that the universe must have come from somewhere, they're just not ready to admit that it's outside of their understanding, so they'll come up with whatever theories they can to get around the obvious.

The bottom line is this: Because of these space-time theorems, we're forced to conclude there must be a God beyond space and time that created the universe.

In other words, Genesis got it right thousands of years ago.

The first sentence of the Bible says that God created the heavens and the Earth. In the next sentence, the Earth already exists, and the narrative goes straight to God's work of creation on Earth. So, it seems as if Genesis describes the creation of the entire universe in one sentence without going into detail as to how that part of creation actually happened.

The obvious question is, what was God doing between the first and second sentences of the Bible?

Genesis may not go into detail on it, but the rest of the Bible does. In fact, there are at least 11 places in the Bible where it tells us that God "stretched out" the heavens.

(Job 9:8, Psalm 104:2, Isaiah 40:22, Isaiah 42:5, Isaiah 44:24, Isaiah 45:12, Isaiah 48:13, Isaiah 51:13, Jeremiah 10:12, Jeremiah 51:15, and Zechariah 12:1)

The English translations in these 11 texts have to do with stretching out the heavens, but the Hebrew word used is "natah" (except in Isaiah 48:13).

This word in Hebrew means the expansion of what's being described.

Synonyms for this word include "extend" or "spread out." This word is used in the Bible in reference to a tent being spread out, so that should help you visualize the meaning of the word.

Think of pitching a tent. It starts as a folded cloth of some kind, and then the cloth is spread out - you might even say it is "expanded" to its fully functional form.

What's interesting is that scientists now believe that our universe is expanding and has been since the beginning of time.

According to Dr. Hugh Ross, no scientist had even dreamt of the idea of an expanding universe until Albert Einstein produced his theory of relativity. Then Edwin Hubble and other scientists also showed that the universe is expanding.

For thousands of years, the Bible stood alone as the only book in science, philosophy, or theology that described the universe as having been expanded.

Now we can see that it was right.

The formation of an abundant, stable water cycle

At first glance, the Bible can seem like an "unscientific" book. This is why some people think there's a clash between science and the Bible. But if you look closely, you'll see that the Bible is filled with explanations of how nature works.

For example, the Bible says in Genesis that God separated the waters below from the waters above. Dr. Hugh Ross says this could be a reference to the atmosphere and the water cycle.

If you go to the book of Job, in chapters 37 and 38, it talks in detail about the water cycle that God established on day 2 of creation. You'll see that the water cycle is set up with 16 types of precipitation, and we need every one of them for life to be possible. The 6 main ones are rain, mist, dew, snow, frost, and hail. Without at least those 6, we wouldn't be able to grow the quantity of crops necessary to sustain a high-technology civilization.

What's interesting is, Earth needs to be massive enough that it doesn't lose water vapor to outer space, but it also needs a thin atmosphere. So whatever God did in this stage of creation, it gave us the mass we needed, the atmosphere we needed, the ocean we needed, and the water cycle we needed.

According to Dr. Ross, the probability of any event "accidentally" giving us a water cycle and a transparent atmosphere without God designing it is less than 1 chance in a trillion trillion trillion trillion.

Our planet has a built-in, life-giving, eerily-consistent sprinkler system that keeps us alive without any help from us. That doesn't happen by accident.

(And the Bible described it thousands of years ago.)

We have to be careful to not jump to conclusions.

The Bible has been put to the test for thousands of years. Investigate before you decide, and you'll find it trustworthy.

Statements Consistent with Astronomy

In addition to the creation narrative, there are a number of other places where science has corroborated the Bible's accuracy.[32]

First, the Bible frequently refers to the great number of stars in the heavens. Here are two examples of the Bible comparing the number of stars to the number of grains of sand on Earth:

- Genesis 22:17 says, "I will multiply your descendants as the stars of the heaven and as the sand which is on the seashore"

- Jeremiah 33:22 says, "As the host of heaven cannot be numbered, nor the sand of the sea measured, so will I multiply the descendants of David My servant and the Levites who minister to Me."

Even today, scientists admit that they do not know exactly how many stars there are. Only about 3,000-5,000 stars can be seen with the naked eye, but there have been estimates of there being as many as 10^{21}.[33]

It doesn't take a mathematician to see that the number of grains of sand on all the seashores on Earth is too much to count. (One very rough estimate puts it at around 7.5×10^{18}.[34]) It's amazing to think that even though only a few thousand stars can be seen with the human eye, the writers of the Bible said they were as innumerable as the sands on the seashores, and now we know they were right.

The Bible also says that each star is unique. 1 Corinthians 15:41 says, "There is one glory of the sun, another glory of the moon, and another glory of the stars; for one star differs from another star in glory."

Stars mostly look alike to the untrained and unmagnified eye. Even when seen through a telescope, they look to simply be points of light. However, analysis of their light spectra reveals that each is unique and different from all others.[35]

The Bible describes the suspension of the Earth in space. Job 26:7 says, "He stretches out the north over empty space; He hangs the earth on nothing." How incredible is it that a person thousands of years ago can make such a bold statement with no technology or space exploration to back it up, yet still be correct? That only makes sense if that person is truly pulling from the Source and Cause of all life.

Statements Consistent with Meteorology

The Bible describes the circulation of the atmosphere. Ecclesiastes 1:6 says, "The wind goes toward the south, and turns around to the north; The wind whirls about continually, and comes again on its circuit."

We now know that atmospheric circulation involves wind moving around in a "circuit," much like descriptions in the ancient biblical text (which the author would have had no way to research). This circulation of wind helps transport energy and heat from the equator to the poles.

How would an ancient writer know these things long before the Earth had been explored and before mass communication existed? There are many educated adults today who don't know this, yet we don't find it incredible that an ancient writer did?

The Bible includes some principles of fluid dynamics. Job 28:25 says, "To establish a weight for the wind, and apportion the waters by measure." The fact that air has weight was proven scientifically only about 300 years ago.[36] The weights of air and water are needed for the efficient functioning of the world's hydrologic cycle, which in turn sustains life on the Earth.

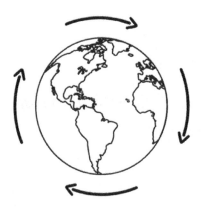

"The wind goes toward the south, and turns around to the north; The wind whirls about continually, and comes again on its circuit."

- The Bible (long before meteorologists existed)

Statements Consistent with Biology

The Bible describes the value of blood. Leviticus 17:11 says, "For the life of a creature is in the blood..." The blood carries water and nourishment to every cell, maintains the body's temperature, and removes the waste material of the body's cells. Blood also carries oxygen from the lungs throughout the body. But it wasn't until the 17th century that William Harvey discovered how blood circulation worked, which led to the understanding of the true purpose and value of blood—confirming what the Bible revealed thousands of years earlier.

The Bible connects mental and physical health. In America today, we are beginning to learn more and more that a person's mental and spiritual health is strongly connected to and correlated with their physical health. The Bible told us this thousands of years ago.

Proverbs 14:30 says, "A sound heart is life to the body, but envy is rottenness to the bones." Proverbs 15:30 says, "The light of the eyes rejoices the heart, and a good report makes the bones healthy." Proverbs 16:24 says, "Pleasant words are like a honeycomb, sweetness to the soul and health to the bones." Proverbs 17:22 says, "A merry heart does good, like medicine, but a broken spirit dries the bones."

> ## The risk of developing some physical illnesses is higher in people with depression [...]The reasons are not yet clear.

- NATIONAL INSTITUTE OF MENTAL HEALTH

(The Bible connected mental and physical health thousands of years ago).

> ## Research also suggests that people with depression are at higher risk for osteoporosis relative to others.

- NATIONAL INSTITUTE OF MENTAL HEALTH

(The Bible says "a broken spirit dries the bones.")

Statements Consistent with Hydrology

The Bible describes the hydrologic cycle.

We've covered it briefly already, but here are some places in the Bible that talk about the water cycle:

Psalm 135:7 says, "He causes the vapors to ascend from the ends of the earth; He makes lightning for the rain; He brings the wind out of His treasuries."

Jeremiah 10:13 says, "When he utters his voice, there is a tumult of waters in the heavens, and he makes the mist rise from the ends of the earth. He makes lightning for the rain, and he brings forth the wind from his storehouses."

Also, Job 36:27-29 says, "For He draws up drops of water, which distill as rain from the mist, which the clouds drop down and pour abundantly on man. Indeed, can anyone understand the spreading of clouds, the thunder from His canopy?"

In these verses, we can see an ancient description of the hydrologic cycle, which is defined as "a continuous exchange of moisture between the oceans, the atmosphere, and the land" and includes processes such as evaporation, atmospheric circulation, condensation, and precipitation, among others.[37]

The drops of water which eventually pour down as rain first become vapor and then condense into tiny liquid water droplets in the clouds. These finally coalesce into drops large enough to overcome the updrafts that suspend them in the air.

And the Bible told us all of this thousands of years ago.

The more I study nature, the more I stand amazed at the work of the Creator.

- LOUIS PASTEUR

**FRENCH CHEMIST
AND MICROBIOLOGIST**

> **God has, in fact, written two books, not just one. Of course, we are all familiar with the first book he wrote, namely Scripture. But he has written a second book called creation.**
>
> **- SIR FRANCIS BACON**
>
> DEVELOPED THE SCIENTIFIC METHOD

The Bible describes the recirculation of water.

Ecclesiastes 1:7 says, "All the rivers run into the sea, Yet the sea is not full; To the place from which the rivers come, There they return again."

Isaiah 55:10 says, "For as the rain comes down, and the snow from heaven, And do not return there, But water the earth, And make it bring forth and bud, That it may give seed to the sower And bread to the eater [...]"

The Bible refers to the surprising amount of water that can be held as condensation in clouds.

Job 26:8 says, "He binds up the water in His thick clouds, Yet the clouds are not broken under it." According to the National Weather Service, "One inch of rain over one square mile equals 17.4 million gallons of water weighing 143 million pounds (about 72,000 tons), or the weight of a train with 40 boxcars."[38]

Hydrothermal vents were described in the Bible thousands of years before their discovery.

Hydrothermal vents are hot springs on the ocean floor, and the Bible talked about them a LONG time before they were discovered in the 1970s.

Genesis 7:11 says, "all the fountains of the great deep were broken up, and the windows of heaven were opened." Job 38:16 says, "Have you entered the springs of the sea? Or have you walked in search of the depths?"

Statements Consistent with Geology

The Bible describes the Earth's crust.

Jeremiah 31:37 says that heavens above can't be measured, and the foundations of the earth below can't be "searched out."

As we've discussed already, we don't know exactly how large the universe actually is, and we also haven't drilled through the Earth's crust. Earth's core is about 4,000 miles beneath the surface, and the furthest we've been able to drill down is just over 7 miles.[39] We've got a long way to go, and between extreme depths, heat, and pressure, we'll be doing really good if we get past the top layer. In other words, the Bible is spot on.

The Bible described the shape of the Earth centuries before people thought that the Earth was round.

Isaiah 40:22 says, "It is He who sits above the circle of the earth, and its inhabitants are like grasshoppers, who stretches out the heavens like a curtain, and spreads them out like a tent to dwell in."

The word translated "circle" here is the Hebrew word which can also be translated as "circuit," or "compass" (depending on the context). That is, it indicates something spherical, rounded, or arched—not something that is flat or square.

The book of Isaiah was most likely written sometime between the 700s and 600s BC. This is at least 300 years before Aristotle suggested that the Earth might be a sphere in this book *On the Heavens*.

> I love to think of nature as unlimited broadcasting stations, through which God speaks to us every day, every hour and every moment of our lives, if we will only tune in and remain so.
>
> **- GEORGE WASHINGTON CARVER**
>
> AMERICAN AGRICULTURAL SCIENTIST

Statements Consistent with Scientific Discovery Regarding Water on Earth

The book of Genesis says that water used to cover the Earth.

Genesis chapter 1, verses 2-3 say:

"The earth was formless and void, and darkness was over the surface of the deep, and the Spirit of God was moving over the surface of the waters. Then God said, 'Let there be light'; and there was light."

Science has now discovered that, at one point in history, the Earth was probably covered in water. Of course, no scientist or researcher can be 100 percent certain, but the idea of a cool, water covered Earth at some point in our planet's history lines up with current scientific findings.[40]

Science has now discovered that at one point in history, the earth was probably covered in water. The Bible said it thousands of years ago.

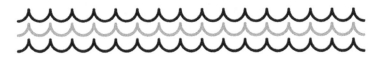

Section 4: Reasons to believe in the Resurrection of Jesus

The resurrection of Jesus Christ is the center of everything in the Bible, and it is the cornerstone of the Christian worldview.

If the resurrection is true, the Bible and everything else Jesus said is also true. Therefore, if the resurrection is true, then life has purpose and meaning beyond anything we could otherwise imagine.

So how can anyone prove that Jesus rose from the dead?

The only acceptable way to "prove" that something happened is by eyewitness testimony and evidence. In courts of law, we talk to people who saw the events in question, and we look at evidence that those events happened. The resurrection of Jesus is subject to the same tests.

In the ancient world, if you have two sources for something, that's a pretty good argument that it happened. That's pretty rare.

For Jesus' resurrection, we have direct written eyewitness testimony from at least 6 sources who saw and testified and lived the rest of their lives in the belief that they saw Jesus risen from the dead.

That doesn't count all the people who were said to have seen Jesus risen from the dead who contributed to the massive growth of Christianity in the years immediately after Jesus' death.

If you counted the first church leaders and members, the number of people who devoted their lives to the belief that Jesus rose from the dead based on eyewitness testimony could easily be counted in the thousands.

If we had that kind of testimony for any event today, or for any other historical event for that matter, we would accept it without a doubt. But because Jesus' resurrection is outside of what we think is possible, we often ignore the evidence.

But let's look at the evidence from the early eyewitnesses.

If the resurrection is true, life has purpose and meaning. And we have a LOT of evidence for the resurrection.

How do we know Jesus existed?

Bart Ehrman, an agnostic historian and professor at the University of North Carolina, once said, "I don't think there's any serious historian who doubts the existence of Jesus."[41]

He went on to say, "There are a lot of people who want to write sensational books and make a lot of money who say Jesus didn't exist, but I don't know any serious scholar who doubts the existence of Jesus."

In another setting, Ehrman (who again, is agnostic) said, "There is no scholar in any college or university in the western world who teaches classics, ancient history, New Testament, early Christianity, (or) any related field, who doubts that Jesus existed."[42]

> ## I don't know any serious scholar who doubts the existence of Jesus.
> ### - PROFESSOR BART EHRMAN (AGNOSTIC)

Those are powerful words. The fact is, Jesus is abundantly attested in early, independent sources, and even skeptical historians like Bart Ehrman concede that.

Ehrman says if you're going to have a different opinion, you better have a pretty good piece of evidence yourself. He says atheists have done themselves a disservice by jumping on the bandwagon of mythicism because it makes them look foolish to the outside world.

Some people insist on reaching desperately by claiming that Jesus didn't exist, but they do so with no evidence whatsoever to back up such a claim. Between Bart Ehrman's statements and the abundance of evidence that will follow in this book, we can rest assured that Jesus of Nazareth did, in fact, exist.

Is the eyewitness testimony reliable?

The most important thing to consider in any case is eyewitness testimony. Who saw the event in question actually happen? If you have people who saw it happen, no matter how unlikely it is, courts will say that's enough to be confident beyond a reasonable doubt.

In the case of Jesus' resurrection, there were many people who saw it. So, the most important question is: Can we rely on the testimony of the eyewitnesses of Jesus' resurrection? Let's look at some possible objections to the reliability of the early eyewitness testimony that said Jesus rose from the dead.

How do we know that the testimony of Jesus rising from the dead isn't just a myth that evolved over time?

Some people claim that the New Testament was written a long time after Jesus' death and therefore is simply mythology that developed over time. If that's true, then the stories of Jesus are simply embellishments that evolved through centuries of wishful thinking.

I personally believed this for a while, but there are some serious problems with this idea, and I've found that most people who believe this do not base their objection on facts.

The truth of the matter is, the Gospels are dated much too early to be mythology.

Even by critical scholars, the Gospels are dated to have been written between AD 70 and AD 95. That's a critical, late date, and it's still only 40-65 years after the events occurred. Even that critical date is still within the lifetimes of people who would have been able to refute the story. Myths don't develop that fast. It takes hundreds of years - multiple generations - for mythology to develop.

But there's good evidence that shows the Gospels were written much earlier than the amount of time it would take for a myth to take root.

The Gospels are dated much too early to be mythology.

Cold Case Christianity Method

The New Testament Does Not Describe the Destruction of the Temple[43]

The New Testament does not mention the siege of Jerusalem in the late 60s AD or the fall of the temple in Jerusalem in AD 70. These were monumental events in ancient history that might be considered similar to the modern-day 9/11 attack or Pearl Harbor. Yet the New Testament, which includes an abundance of historical details throughout, never once mentions this huge event in Jewish history.

Considering the fact that Jesus predicted the fall of the temple in the book of Matthew, it would only make sense for the writers to mention it if that prediction had actually happened at the time of their writing. Instead, no New Testament document mentions it.

The only explanation for this is that these books were written before all of that happened.

Luke Did Not Mention the Deaths of Paul, Peter, and James

Paul was the main character in the book of Acts, and Acts ends with Paul being under house arrest in Rome. Writings from early church fathers tell us that Paul died in the 60s AD during persecution from Emperor Nero.

Peter was also martyred shortly after Paul in the AD 60s. While Luke wrote extensively about Paul and Peter in the book of Acts and featured them prominently, he said nothing about their deaths. After all, Paul was still alive (under house arrest in Rome) at the end of the book of Acts.

So, the logical conclusion is that Acts was written before Paul and Peter died. That puts Acts as being written before the 60s AD.

James was also killed in the city of Jerusalem in the 60s AD, and his execution is also absent from the biblical account, even though Luke described the deaths of Stephen (Acts 7:54–60) and James, the brother of John (Acts 12:1–2).

Acts was part two of a two-part series from Luke, and part one was what we know as the Gospel of Luke. Acts starts out with reference to the first writing, Luke's gospel, which means the Gospel of Luke must have been written before the 60s AD as well.

Paul Quoted Luke's Gospel in His Letter to Timothy and in his letter to the Corinthians

Paul appeared to be aware of Luke's gospel when he quoted it in his letter to Timothy around AD 63–64. Paul said:

> For the Scripture says, "You shall not muzzle the ox while he is threshing," and "The laborer is worthy of his wages." (1 Timothy 5:17–18)

In the above verse, Paul quotes two passages as "Scripture" - one in the Old Testament and one in the New Testament.

The line that says "the laborer is worthy of his wages" points back to Luke 10:7. So we can clearly see that Luke's gospel must have been common knowledge and considered Scripture, at least to Paul, by the AD 60s.

Paul also shows familiarity with Luke's gospel in his letter to the Corinthian church nearly ten years earlier than his letter to Timothy. Here's what Paul said:

> For I received from the Lord that which I also delivered to you, that the Lord Jesus in the night in which He was betrayed took bread; and when He had given thanks, He broke it and said, "This is My body, which is for you; do this in remembrance of Me." In the same way He took the cup also after supper, saying, "This cup is the new covenant in My blood." (1 Corinthians 11:23–25)

Luke 22:19-20 says essentially the same thing:

> And when He had taken some bread and given thanks, He broke it and gave it to them, saying, "This is My body which is given for you; do this in remembrance of Me." And in the same way He took the cup after they had eaten, saying, "This cup which is poured out for you is the new covenant in My blood.

Luke's gospel is the only one that says, "do this in remembrance of me." So again, Paul seems to be quoting Luke's gospel. Where else would he have gotten the exact same words Luke used? Either way, either Luke's gospel or the source of Luke's gospel information clearly predates Paul's messages to the churches he planted, which was at least in the AD 60s.

Myths take hundreds of years to develop. The Gospels were written **in the same generation** of the events they described. Myths don't develop that fast.

Greek myths evolved over centuries of oral tradition.

Luke Quoted Mark and Matthew Repeatedly

Luke admitted at the beginning of his own gospel that he was not an eyewitness to the life and ministry of Jesus. Instead, Luke described himself as a person who was simply collecting information from eyewitnesses:

> Inasmuch as many have undertaken to compile an account of the things accomplished among us, just as they were handed down to us by those who from the beginning were eyewitnesses and servants of the word, it seemed fitting for me as well, having investigated everything carefully from the beginning, to write it out for you in consecutive order, most excellent Theophilus; so that you may know the exact truth about the things you have been taught. (Luke 1:1–4)

Because of the nature of Luke's purpose, research, and writing, Luke often repeated or quoted entire passages from the gospels of Mark and Matthew.

In fact, Luke quoted about 350 verses from Mark and about 250 verses from Matthew.

The logical conclusion is that Mark's account was already written and available to Luke prior to writing his own gospel. If Luke's gospel was written in the 60's AD or earlier, then that places Mark's gospel as being written even earlier than that.

It may be taken as historically certain that Peter and the disciples had experiences after Jesus's death in which Jesus appeared to them as the risen Christ.

- GERD LÜDEMANN (AGNOSTIC)

**GERMAN NEW TESTAMENT
SCHOLAR AND HISTORIAN**

Based on these facts, we can piece together an estimated timeline for when the stories of Jesus' resurrection began circulating:

- The deaths of Paul, Peter, and James were all in the AD 60s, and the destruction of the temple was in AD 70. None of the events are mentioned in the book of Acts despite the fact that Acts is all about Paul, Peter, and James' work and despite the fact that the destruction of the temple was the most significant event in Jewish culture at that time. This leads us to conclude that Acts must have been written before the AD 60s.

- The book of Acts was the second part of Luke's writing. The first part was the Gospel of Luke, which means Luke's gospel was written before the AD 60s.

- Paul quoted Luke's gospel in his letters written in the AD 50s, so the Gospel of Luke must have been written by that time.

- Luke's gospel quotes the Gospel of Mark repeatedly, so Mark's gospel must have been around before the AD 50s.

- That puts the earliest gospel account we know of today - the Gospel of Mark - as being written by no later than the late AD 40s or early 50s. Jesus died in the AD 30s, so that means the story of Jesus' resurrection was circulating within a decade of his death.

Skeptics typically date Mark's gospel to around 70 AD. Anything earlier than that implies that miracles are possible due to the fact that Jesus predicted the fall of the temple, and it fell in AD 70. So, the non-Christian worldview must start its timeline after the temple fell, or they admit that it's true. It's interesting how that works.

The truth is, either Matthew, Paul, Peter, James, John, and Jude were all lying when they wrote their books of the New Testament - either they were all in on the same giant pointless conspiracy and dedicated their lives to it without faltering - or they were simply telling what they had seen and heard.

I personally think the latter makes more sense.

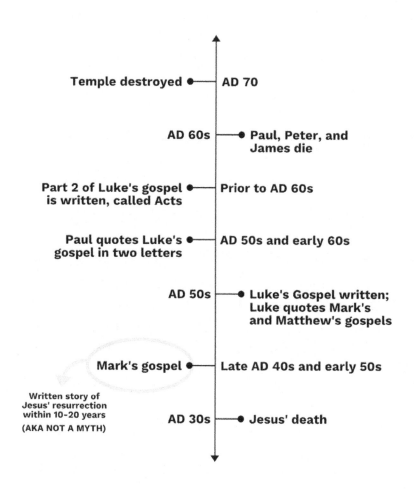

Temple destroyed • AD 70

AD 60s •—— Paul, Peter, and
James die

Part 2 of Luke's gospel •—— Prior to AD 60s
is written, called Acts

Paul quotes Luke's •—— AD 50s and early 60s
gospel in two letters

AD 50s •—— Luke's Gospel written;
Luke quotes Mark's
and Matthew's gospels

Mark's gospel •—— Late AD 40s and early 50s

**Written story of
Jesus' resurrection
within 10-20 years
(AKA NOT A MYTH)**

AD 30s •—— Jesus' death

Minimal Facts Argument

Here's another way to tell that the New Testament was written early and wasn't a myth that developed over time. This research comes from Dr. Gary Habermas.[44]

Many skeptics critique the Gospels, but they generally like Paul's writings and think he's a good source because:

He was an authority, a scholar, a Jewish leader and teacher, he was in the right place at the right time, he knew the apostles, he persecuted the church, he was a brilliant man, and he was honest.

Of Paul's writings, critics generally agree on 7 of the 13 books that bear his name: Romans, 1 Corinthians, 2 Corinthians, Galatians, Philippians, 1 Thessalonians, and Philemon.

Most skeptical scholars will acknowledge that 1 Corinthians and Galatians were both letters written by Paul in the 50s AD. Based solely on 1 Corinthians chapter 15 and Galatians chapters 1 & 2, we can see that the belief that Jesus rose from the dead was a very early belief.

1 Corinthians chapter 15 says:

> *For I delivered to you as of first importance what I also received, that Christ died for our sins according to the Scriptures, and that He was buried, and that He was raised on the third day according to the Scriptures, and that He appeared to Cephas, then to the twelve. After that He appeared to more than five hundred brethren at one time, most of whom remain until now, but some have fallen asleep; then He appeared to James, then to all the apostles;*

and last of all, as to one untimely born, He appeared to me
also.

This was written in the 50s AD. Apparently, this is the message Paul was using when he started the church in Corinth, and he must have used the same message when he started the other churches (like the church in Galatia), because he started the churches in Corinth and in Galatia around the same time (early 50s AD according to Acts and based on the fact that Paul wrote letters to both churches around the same time in the mid-50s AD).

Then, in the book of Galatians, Paul gives us a timeline of what happened after his conversion, and he gives us an idea as to when and how he got the message he was spreading (the "Gospel").

Paul basically says this:

He was converted when Jesus appeared to him (post-resurrection) while he (Paul) was on his way to persecute Christians. Then he says he waited a few years before consulting with anyone about the revelation he had.

So, 3 years after his experience with Jesus, he went to Jerusalem to *interview* Peter (the Greek word used by Paul means to gain knowledge by visiting).

Then, 14 years later, he went back to Jerusalem to double-check the gospel he had been spreading and was told that everything was still good with his message. So, he went out to spread the gospel among the Gentiles (see Galatians chapters 1 and 2).

Do the math. If Paul wrote Galatians and 1 Corinthians in the AD 50s, and we work that timeline backward, here's our timeline:

- Mid 50s AD: Paul wrote 1 Corinthians and Galatians

- Sometime before Paul wrote Galatians in the 50s: Paul double-checks the gospel in Jerusalem to make sure nothing had changed in the message they were sharing

- 14 years prior to that (at least 40 AD, probably earlier) - Paul visits Jerusalem and interviews Peter before starting to spread the good news. Where else would he have gotten the message of Jesus' resurrection that he was preaching when he began starting churches in the years after this meeting with Peter?

So, Paul was traveling and preaching the message that Jesus rose from the dead, and he tells us in Galatians (written in the AD 50s) that he got that message at least 14 years prior to him writing his letter to the Galatians.

At the very least, we're back at the news of Jesus rising from the dead being spread within a decade or so of Jesus' death.

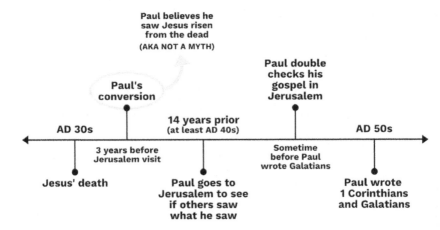

If Paul checked his original message with James and Peter, that means they had it before Paul had it, which means this creed goes back even before Paul's receiving it. The creed Paul recites in 1 Corinthians (which he said he also received) was in a standardized form in Greek when Paul received it, and it would have taken a while to put eyewitness testimony in a standardized form. Now we're almost all the way back to the event of Jesus' death.

So, James and Peter had a testimony, and they standardized it into a creed that was easier to remember. Paul hears it and then passes this creed along to the church in Corinth in 51-52 AD.

Paul tells us in his letter to the Galatians that his initial revelation came from God, and the information he was sharing (about Jesus rising from the dead) was double-checked by Peter and James on two occasions over the course of 14 years.

The letters to the Corinthians and to the Galatians were written in the 50s AD. That tells us that Paul's beliefs of the resurrected Jesus - which he apparently had been carrying around for a long time - were given to him within just a few years of the cross.

James D.G. Dunn, one of the most established historical Jesus scholars in the world, says that the latest this standardized creed form could have come about is months after the cross.

Larry Hurtado, another scholar, says that it came out in that standardized form just days after the cross. And why not? It was the central Christian message, and they needed it in a form that would make it easy for illiterate people to remember. After all, many sociologists of religion believe that up to 90% of Jesus' audience was illiterate. Illiterate people can remember a song or a hymn because it's in a form that's easy to remember. That's how early creeds were structured.

So, as soon as Jesus died in 30 AD, these 3 facts were there:

- Jesus died

- He was raised from the dead

- And he's God in human form

Here's a more exact timeline, according to Habermas:

- 55 AD - Paul wrote 1 Corinthians

- 51 AD - Paul preached at Corinth

- 35 AD - Paul met Peter and James in Jerusalem (Peter must have gotten this empty tomb idea from somewhere so soon after Jesus' death. The Gospels say he was an eyewitness along with hundreds of other people.)

- 32 AD - Paul converted - Jesus appears to him

- 30 AD - Jesus died on the cross

No matter what the exact dates are, the implication is huge: Within *just a few years* of Jesus' death, Paul was preaching that Jesus had risen from the dead and appeared to several eyewitnesses. No matter how you spin it, the message of Jesus' resurrection started early. It wasn't a myth that evolved over time.

But let's go with a critical view for a moment and say that it did take 10 years or so for the message to start spreading. Do you remember what happened 10-20 years ago? Of course. I do, too.

Imagine someone telling you that there was a man in your city who could fly, and he did so in the year 2000 (about 20 years ago). It would be very easy to check this claim, being that you lived in the area during that time and would probably know plenty of people you could ask to corroborate or refute the story. Plus, the story going around in this example (and in the case of the resurrection of Jesus) isn't an ordinary one. It isn't exactly something people could have missed. If someone were doing something as amazing as what you're told, you would have some idea as to whether or not this was true.

Add commitment to the mix (the truth of the resurrection meant giving your life to this belief), and now people would be much more incentivized to investigate the validity of these claims. And they would have easily been able to do so.

That was the scenario in Jerusalem and all Judea after Jesus died, and yet the idea that Jesus rose from the dead spread like wildfire over the next decade and throughout the following century. That only happens if people have strong evidence to lean on, which they obviously did. The bottom line is, the New Testament was written right after the events happened, and myths can't develop that quickly.

Do you remember what happened 10-20 years ago? Me, too.
Myths can't spread that soon.

Chain of Custody: Further Evidence that the Gospel Didn't Change Over Time

Here's what J. Warner Wallace of Cold Case Christianity calls the New Testament chain of custody:[45]

- Jesus' ministry was around 30-33 AD.

- John followed Jesus and wrote the Gospel of John.

- Ignatius, Polycarp, and Papias were students of John that became church leaders, and we have their letters and writings.

- Irenaeus was another church leader after Ignatius, Polycarp, and Papias, and we have his writings as well.

- Hippolytus (around AD 200) came after Irenaeus, and we have his writings, too.

For all of these church leaders, we have several books worth of writings, and they all tell the same basic facts as the Gospels. And there are other chains of custody for Paul's and Peter's writing as well.

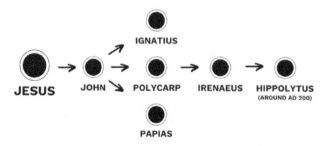

SAME EXACT MESSAGE

What's important to note is that these 3 eyewitnesses – Paul, John, and Peter – and their students were in 3 different geographical regions (Rome for Paul, Asia Minor or Ephesus for John, and North Africa for Peter).

If you lost the entire New Testament and only had the writings of the first "officers" in the chain of custody, here's what you would know about Jesus:

- Born of a virgin

- Worked miracles

- Preached sermons

- Claimed to be God

- Was worshipped as God

- Was crucified and buried

- Rose from the dead

- Ascended into Heaven

- By faith alone you are saved

And you get all of that just from the writings that were being passed down from the time of the eyewitnesses until the time of the church councils in AD 363 when the New Testament canon was officially established.

EARLY

OFTEN

CONSISTENT

The message of Jesus we have today was described early, repeated often, and it never changed.

So, the message of the Gospel - that Jesus rose from the dead - started early and didn't change over time.

Whether you choose to believe that the message of Jesus' resurrection started spreading via the Gospels immediately after Jesus' death or 50 years later, the truth remains the same:

Several eyewitnesses claimed and lived by the fact that they saw Jesus resurrected.

Whichever way you choose to believe, keep this in mind:

Memoirs of World War 2 weren't done until the 1990s (50 years after the fact). Were they liars?

What about Alexander the Great? According to Dr. Habermas, the earliest good source we have for Alexander is 350 years after his death (he died in 330 BC). The two best biographies on him didn't come until 425-450 years after his death.

Writing takes time, especially in a culture where the written word is not the primary means of mass communication. Not many people could read or write in Jesus' time, so why rush to write a book about something you saw?

So, whether you believe it's 2 years or 50 years, the facts remain the same, and the proof is still just as evident.

Now, it is interesting and significant - isn't it? - that a historian setting forth in that spirit, without any theological bias whatever, should find that he simply cannot portray the progress of humanity honestly without giving a foremost place to a peniless teacher from Nazareth.

- H.G. WELLS, WRITER AND HISTORIAN

(WHEN ASKED WHO WAS THE
GREATEST PERSON IN HISTORY)

Aren't the copies we have of the New Testament and the Gospels from much later?

Christians typically say that there are 25,000 New Testament manuscripts, but skeptics sometimes point out that the vast majority of those manuscripts came centuries later. They might also claim that we actually don't have many manuscripts at all from the first few centuries after Jesus' death.

The thing is, no matter how many early manuscripts there are (and there are plenty of them), we have the letters from the early church fathers written in the early 2nd-century (still within 100 years of Jesus' death) that quote almost the entire New Testament.

These were letters that were written and handed down meticulously for each new generation from the time of Jesus' death, and the central message is the same. We don't see the "telephone game" happening (the game where kids whisper something to the kid sitting next to them and the message is passed along in that manner until it goes all the way around the room only to find that the message is completely different at the end). The whisper game effect involves speaking at very low levels - that's what makes it funny. The gospel spread loudly and clearly, and historical documents show that it didn't change.

And all of this is really irrelevant because we know from early non-Christian sources that the Christian church was spreading like crazy within just a few years of Jesus' death, and we know that their primary belief was that Jesus rose from the dead.

The answer to this objection is that we do have a ton of writing from early manuscripts, but we also have writings from 1st and 2nd-century church leaders, and we have writings from non-Christian sources all within one century of Jesus' death that all corroborate the New Testament Gospels.

And even if we didn't have that abundant amount of early information, we would still have the fact that the Christian church exploded to the point where the Roman emperor himself was persecuting Christians just 30 years after Jesus' death.

So, the question we can't avoid is: Why did all those people believe Jesus rose from the dead immediately after His death?

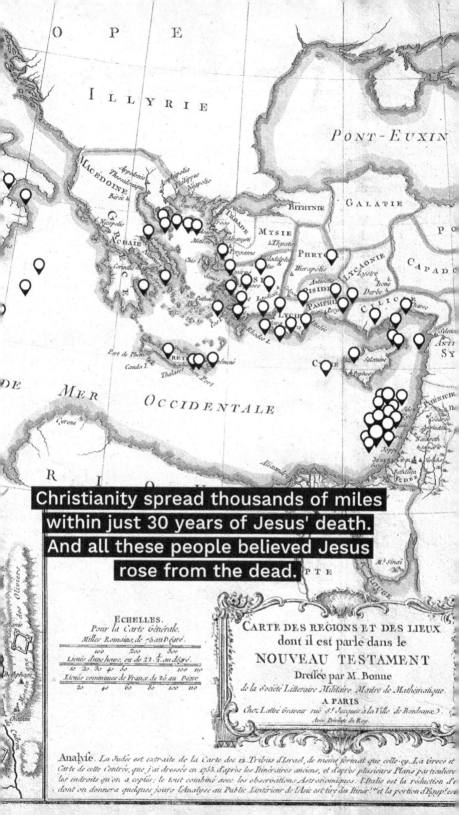

Christianity spread thousands of miles within just 30 years of Jesus' death. And all these people believed Jesus rose from the dead.

CARTE DES REGIONS ET DES LIEUX
dont il est parlé dans le
NOUVEAU TESTAMENT
Dressée par M. Bonne
de la Société Littéraire Militaire, Maître de Mathématique.
A PARIS
Chez Lattré Graveur rue St. Jacques à la Ville de Bordeaux.
Avec Privilège du Roy.

ECHELLES.
Pour la Carte Générale.
Milles Romains, de 75 au Degré.
Lieües d'une heure, ou de 22 ½ au Degré.
Lieües communes de France de 25 au Degré.

Analyse. La Judée est extraite de la Carte des 12 Tribus d'Israel, de même format que celle-cy. La Grèce et Carte de cette Contrée, que j'ai dressée en 1755, d'après les Itineraires anciens, et d'après plusieurs Plans particuliers les endroits qu'on a copiés; le tout combiné avec les observations Astronomiques. L'Italie est la réduction d'u dont on donnera quelques jours l'Analyse au Public. L'intérieur de l'Asie est tiré des Itiner.et la portion d'Egypt'es

Even if we have early manuscripts, how do we know they're not just fiction literature?

The disciples devoted their lives to spreading the message that Jesus rose from the dead. As we've already covered, Paul's letters from the AD 50s show us that.

Some skeptics might say, "More manuscripts at best increase our confidence that we have the original version. That doesn't mean the original copy was history — just like the original copy of *The Wizard of Oz* or the Arthurian legends wouldn't be a record of history."

The problem with that line of thinking is that people didn't instantly dedicate their lives to either of those pieces of fictional literature. They did instantly start following Jesus as the risen Son of God. That speaks volumes for what people thought about the gospel.

Christianity spread rapidly in the Roman empire. Non-Christian historical sources tell us that the Roman emperor, Emperor Nero, was persecuting Christians in Rome in the AD 60s. These people were burned alive for holding their beliefs about Jesus, so that shows us that they obviously believed that Jesus' resurrection was a real historical event - not fiction.

Maybe the eyewitnesses hallucinated.

To say that the eyewitnesses of Jesus' resurrection hallucinated goes 100% against everything science and psychology know about hallucinations.

Hallucinations happen to individuals, not groups. They're not contagious. The eyewitnesses were groups of people, men and women, indoors and outdoors, believers and non-believers, etc. On top of that, they heard *and* saw Jesus, so that would have to be auditory and visual hallucinations at the same time, which are even rarer.

Not to mention, the Gospels say that Mary touched Jesus, Jesus ate with multiple people and broke bread with them, and He told Thomas and the other disciples to touch His wounds if they didn't believe Him, which implies they also touched Jesus.

So, you've got 3 types of hallucinations happening at the same time to groups of people in all different scenarios and all different mindsets. That completely goes against current scientific knowledge of hallucinations.

Let's look at this a bit closer for a moment:

- Mary saw Jesus.

- Peter saw Jesus.

- James saw Jesus.

- Paul saw Jesus, and he had no reason at all to want to see Jesus.

- The 2 disciples saw Jesus on the road to Emmaus.

- The women (more than one) at the tomb saw Jesus.

- 10 disciples without Thomas saw Jesus.

- 11 disciples (with Thomas) saw Jesus again.

  ○ They also all saw Jesus at the mountaintop in Matthew 28

  ○ They saw Jesus at His ascension in Luke 24

- 7 of those disciples saw Jesus while they were fishing, too.

- Paul says that 500 people saw Jesus at one time.

More than one person saw Jesus at the same time. Group dreams are not a real thing; that's called a memory of something that actually happened.

Then, if you wanted to falsify this in 1st-century Jerusalem, all you would have to do is check the tomb for Jesus' body. Yet no one produced Jesus' body.

Hallucinations are described by the medical community as something that occurs as a result of some type of psychological disorder, drug use, sleep deprivation, or some type of medical cause such as tumors, fevers, disorders, etc.

In a study of 31,000 "normal" people (people without known disorders) from 18 different countries, only 5% or so of them had experienced at least one hallucination, and only about 3-4% of them reported having experienced more than one hallucination.[46, 47]

Of the total 31,000 people in the study, only 1.6% of them said they experienced more than one type of hallucination or delusion.

If you multiply the 4% of people who experienced **more than one hallucination** by the 1.6% of people who experienced **more than one type of hallucination** (audible, visual, delusional, etc.), you will get a tiny, tiny percentage of people who fall in both categories, and that's including both hallucinations and delusions.

How likely is it then, medically speaking, that at LEAST 13 people saw AND heard Jesus alive in different times, places, and environments?

Some of them touched Jesus as well, so that adds another layer of improbability for hallucinations as an explanation. Plus, as far as we know from ancient writings, none of those people showed signs of being on drugs or having any medical disorders. Therefore, claiming that the disciples hallucinated is farfetched at best.

Hallucinations do not occur naturally in healthy people without psychological disorders.

- DARTMOUTH UNDERGRADUATE JOURNAL OF SCIENCE

Maybe the eyewitnesses lied.

If the eyewitnesses of the resurrection lied, why would they dedicate their lives to a lie and then travel around spreading a major movement suffering tremendous hardships in the process? After all, they claimed to have seen the resurrection firsthand, which means they would have *known* whether or not what they were saying was a lie.

The idea that the disciples lied makes zero sense.

They gained nothing by spending their lives spreading the gospel.

They were excommunicated from the synagogue; then, they were beaten, tortured, and killed.

That's not exactly appealing.

In fact, they had every reason to say the resurrection did *not* happen.

Sure, some of them had a certain level of authority because of their positions, but that authority was really more of a target on their heads than anything.

Most of us struggle with dedicating our lives to causes we know are good, so how likely do you think it is that the 1st-century disciples of Jesus were willing to dedicate their lives to something they knew was false?

People do really stupid things for fame, but not many people are willing to give up their entire life to legitimately suffer both physically and mentally to the point of public ridicule and death for a brief amount of moderate fame.

And there's not a single source saying the disciples lived anything other than lives of deprivation as a result of their testimonies.

Plus, to pull off a conspiracy of this magnitude, there would need to be a level of sophistication that a rag-tag bunch of 1st-century blue-collared workers weren't likely to possess.

A lie of that magnitude was simply too bold of a claim, too close in proximity to the events in question, too elaborate, too risky, and too reward-less to make any sense. The evidence for a conspiracy just isn't there.

Big lies are very difficult to keep going, even if you have power and resources.

The early disciples didn't have the power, money, sophistication or motive to pull off a lie of that magnitude.

(See: Watergate, 1970s)

According to J. Warner Wallace, conspiracies require:

- **A small number of conspirators** - There were at least 11 of them who would have known the truth.

- **A short conspiracy timespan** - The gospel spread for decades after the death of Jesus.

- **Excellent communication between co-conspirators** - They were separated by thousands of miles.

- **Strong familial relationships** - They were mostly men from all walks of life. Most of them were not family and had no real motivation to lie for each other. Why would they be willing to suffer and potentially die for someone they barely knew if it was all a lie?

- **Little or no pressure to confess** - They got all kinds of pressure. They were beaten and persecuted for what they said they believed.

Yet not one of the eyewitnesses ever recanted his or her testimony.

Not to mention, the disciples said that women were the first witnesses of the resurrection. At this time in history, women could testify in hearings, but they weren't considered to be as reliable as men. If you're going to lie about something as huge as Jesus resurrecting from the dead in 1st-century Jerusalem, putting women as your primary witnesses of the initial event isn't the smartest thing you could do.

Now, be realistic for a moment. Why would they want to lie? There was no motive. They gained nothing from it. And it's ridiculous to think they would be able to pull off a lie that big even if they wanted to.

Jesus' disciples gained nothing & gave up everything by spending their lives spreading the news that Jesus rose from the dead.

Why would they die for something they knew was a lie?

Some skeptics say that plenty of people die for their beliefs, so there's nothing special about the fact that the disciples died for theirs. That doesn't make it true.

Here's the difference: People die all the time for things they're told are true, but they don't willingly die for what they *know* is a lie.

What makes the New Testament unique is that the early groups of eyewitnesses would have been in the position to actually know whether or not the resurrection was a lie.

Martyrs die all the time, but they give their life for something they believe to be true based on what *other people* have told them. The early disciples suffered and died for something that was based on what they claimed to have actually seen and experienced for themselves.

Peter, John, James, Paul, and others lived lives of suffering and ultimately died for what they claimed to have seen *firsthand*, not something they were told.

They were in a unique position to actually know if what they were suffering for was the truth or a lie. That's the best evidence you can get.

Muslim martyrs, for example, have no evidence that they'll receive their reward for sacrificing themselves. They die for what they believe to be true, but they have no way of knowing whether or not they're wrong. The early disciples did. They knew if they were telling the truth or not, and they hung their hat on what they saw with their own eyes.

People typically want to know if there are "non-Christian" writers outside the New Testament that tell us about Jesus. The answer is yes, but that's really an irrelevant question. What makes "non-Christian" writers more trustworthy than Christian eyewitnesses? Their testimony is all-the-more powerful because they saw it firsthand.

If you say the Christian writers were biased, then what were they biased against? What reason did they have to lie about Jesus rising from the dead? What did they gain? Nothing.

Think about it. If Jesus was really who He said He was, shouldn't everyone who came into contact with Him be "biased"?

After all, if the people who were around Him were able to walk away "unbiased," what would that say about Jesus' authenticity?

That's like saying you can't get directions to Alaska from people who have been to Alaska because they're biased. The truth is, everyone is biased. Jews that survived the Holocaust were DEFINITELY biased, but that didn't make their testimony any less true.

If anything, the testimony of early Christians should be much more valuable, because they had everything to lose by claiming that Jesus rose from the dead. They literally gained nothing by making those claims, yet everything we know about their lives tells us they never once recanted their testimonies.

What makes Jesus' resurrection unique is that the groups of eyewitnesses would have actually been in the position to know whether or not the resurrection was a lie.

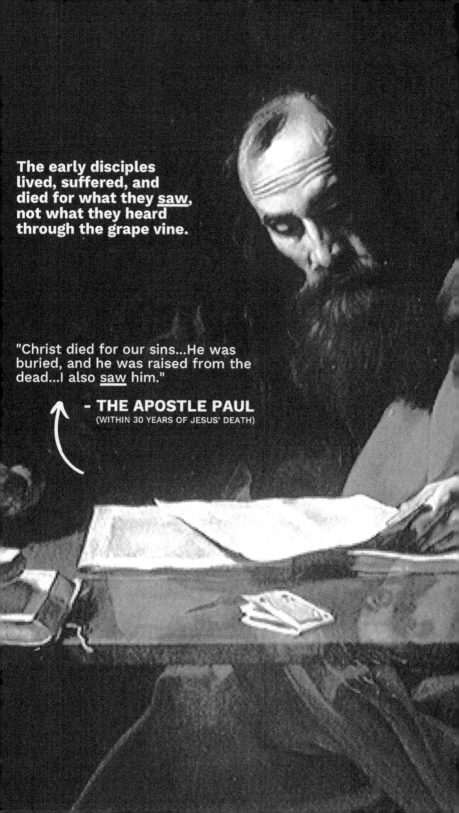

The early disciples
lived, suffered, and
died for what they <u>saw</u>,
not what they heard
through the grape vine.

"Christ died for our sins...He was
buried, and he was raised from the
dead...I also <u>saw</u> him."

- THE APOSTLE PAUL
(WITHIN 30 YEARS OF JESUS' DEATH)

Embarrassing Testimony

When it comes to authenticity, if you find something embarrassing to the author in the text, the chances are higher that it's not going to be invented. After all, not many people lie to make themselves look *bad*. The New Testament documents are filled with embarrassing details about the authors and even about Jesus.

The disciples depict themselves as dimwitted by failing to understand what Jesus is saying in His teachings. They are careless. They fall asleep on Jesus twice when He needs them the most. They make no effort to give Jesus a proper burial after His death. Instead, they let a Jewish leader (the ones who had Jesus killed in the first place) bury Jesus while they ran away and hid.

They are rebuked by Jesus on multiple occasions. At one point, Jesus calls Peter the devil (Mark 8:33), then Jesus has to rebuke and correct the disciples repeatedly for various reasons.

Why make themselves look bad if they're making all this up?

They are cowards. Peter denied Christ 3 times. The disciples all run away when Jesus is killed, and the women are the brave ones. As we've discussed, in that culture, a woman's testimony was not on par with that of a man, yet all 4 Gospels say the women were the first witnesses.

They are doubters. Despite being taught several times that Jesus was going to rise from the dead, they are still doubtful when they hear of His resurrection. Some are even doubtful after they see Him risen.

Jesus' own family thought He was out of His mind (Mark 3:21, 31). Why put this kind of thing in the Bible if they're embellishing Him as God?

Jesus was deserted by many of His followers. In John, chapter 6, Jesus tells His disciples they must eat His flesh and drink His blood (metaphorically), and many disciples deserted Him after that. Why would they even mention this potentially odd and awkward exchange about eating flesh and drinking blood if it's made up?

Jesus was not believed by His own brothers (John 7:5). James, Jesus' brother, later died as a martyr, but he didn't believe Jesus while He was alive.

Jesus is thought to be a deceiver (John 7:12). He turns Jewish believers off to the point where they want to stone Him (John 8:30-59). Jesus is called a "madman" (John 10:20), a "drunkard" (Matthew 11:19), and "demon-possessed" (Mark 3:22, John 7:20, 8:48)

Jesus has His feet wiped with the hair of a prostitute (Luke 7:36-39). This could have easily been seen as a sexual advance. There are also 2 prostitutes in Jesus' bloodline.

Jesus is crucified despite the fact that anyone who was hung on a tree was under God's curse, according to the Jewish Scriptures (Deuteronomy 21:23). If you're making up a Messiah to the Jews, it wouldn't be wise to tell everyone that He hung on a tree.

If you find something that's embarrassing to the author in their writing, it's more likely that they're telling the truth.

And the New Testament is filled with embarrassing details about the writers and about Jesus.

Excruciating Testimony

The word "excruciating" literally means "out of the crucifixion." The people who were in a position to know whether or not Jesus rose from the dead lived brutal lives and died excruciating deaths. They could have spared themselves all of that by simply saying that Jesus didn't rise from the dead, but they didn't. Instead, they held their beliefs, and they even went so far as to change their sacred religious traditions.

Here's what they believed before Christ:

- Animal sacrifice

- Binding Law of Moses

- Strict Monotheism

- The Sabbath

- Conquering Messiah

- Circumcision

Here's what they believed after Christ:

- Christ's sacrifice

- Christ's life

- Trinity

- Sunday Worship (no more Sabbath rules)

- Sacrificial Messiah

- Baptism and Communion

What could have caused these New Testament writers, who were all Jews who already believed they had a relationship with God, to change all of these things virtually overnight?

It can only be explained by what psychologists call an "impact event."

An impact event is an event that is so significant that we can vividly remember details about that event, and that experience ultimately shapes our lives. The apostles must have experienced an impact event to make them change everything so dramatically.

Maybe they were wrong. Maybe Jesus didn't die.

Some people believe that Jesus didn't actually die from crucifixion. After all, Jesus did die in a seemingly short amount of time after being put on the cross. But let's look at the facts.

Before going to the cross, Luke wrote that Jesus prayed so intensely that he started sweating blood. This confused everyone at the time. Some early writers even tried to skip over this when they wrote about it. As it turns out, however, this is actually a medical condition called psychogenic hematidrosis[48], and we now have documented clinical cases where people have experienced this same thing.

Similarly, another initially confusing event is described in the Gospel of John just before the guards removed Jesus from the cross.

Before removing him from the cross, the soldiers pierced Jesus' side, and John's gospel (remember, John is a fisherman) says blood and water flowed out. Early church fathers wrote about this and were confused by it, so they made up all kinds of things to help explain it. However, this is actually a result of pleural effusion[49], which is when water collects around the lower part of the lungs. This can be caused by trauma, among other things.

Jesus' path to the cross was more brutal than most. He was beaten and tortured. They scourged him with a whip with nine tails that had rock or bone at the end. So, the fact that he died relatively quickly should come as no surprise.

In the 1st century, people buried their own, so they were familiar with dead bodies. When people die, their bodies get cold, they get stiff, and they bruise. This is not something that the people from Jesus' time were very likely to have missed.

Not to mention the fact that in ancient history, we're lucky if we have one or two sources to confirm a fact. But in the case of the execution of Jesus Christ, we have multiple early reports from the 1st century in the documents that make up the New Testament and in at least 5 ancient sources outside the Bible that all confirm His execution (Josephus, Tacitus, Lucian, Mara Bar Serapion, and The Jewish Talmud).

SEEING IS BELIEVING

None of the disciples would have had the motive or the ability to convince a skeptical crowd to believe something as wild as a resurrection, unless of course they <u>saw</u> something that conviced them.

70-year-old Jack LaLanne swam handcuffed and shackled for a mile while towing 70 rowboats. People have to see things like that to believe them.

Maybe they were fooled by a fake resurrected Jesus.

In order to con someone, you have to know more about the topic than they do. In order to con the 12, someone would have to know more about Jesus than the 12, and who would know more about Jesus than them? That means it would have to be one of the 12 or someone close to them. To pretend to be Jesus resurrected, they would also have to perform miracles. As you can see, this theory falls apart pretty quickly.

Maybe they were influenced.

Maybe one of them saw a spiritual vision of Jesus and then convinced the others it actually happened. First of all, why would any of them do this just to live a life of suffering and discomfort for something they knew to be a lie? There was nothing to gain from this. But beyond the simple question of why, who could have had this kind of influence to convince everyone, and how could they have pulled off this level of deception among an already skeptical crowd?

Mary? She couldn't even convince Peter, much less Thomas and the others. Plus, she was a woman, which didn't bode well for her at this time in history.

Peter? He was seldom alone, and he didn't have the first vision, Mary did. Did he tell Mary that she saw Jesus the day before he saw Jesus? That doesn't make sense.

Paul? He didn't have influence with the 12, and he came along after the fact.

And even if one of the disciples did have the desire and ability to pull off something as wild as that, it doesn't explain Paul's conversion and vision. Plus, if you were to ask someone like Peter what he saw in his "vision," it would be detailed and vivid. But when he tells others and they tell other people, their descriptions aren't going to be nearly as detailed or vivid, because it would have been Peter's vision. However, the accounts in Scripture are from multiple sources, they contain extensive detail, and they all vary from one another slightly. That's not something you can fake.

Then on top of it all, if you wanted to falsify this person's vision, you would just need to check the tomb. If the tomb is empty, you're back to a conspiracy theory.

It's possible, but not reasonable.

Or maybe they were accurate.

This explains the evidence best.

However, it has strengths and weaknesses. It requires a resurrection, of course, and for naturalists, that's impossible because of their presuppositions. Ask yourself, do you believe supernatural events are possible? You have to get past your presupposition that a resurrection *can't* occur. Otherwise, all the evidence in the world won't mean a thing, and you'll find a way to get around truly believing in the resurrection.

Jesus either rose from the dead or He didn't. Rejecting supernaturalism is the only barricade that will block you from going down the road that leads to the resurrection as a conclusion.

If the Bible is inspired and flawless, Jesus rose from the dead. If it's slightly inspired with a few flaws, Jesus still rose from the dead. If the Bible's not inspired at all, but it's a fairly accurate history book, Jesus still rose from the dead. If the Bible is not inspired, not reliable, and not even a history book (basically just mythology), Jesus still rose from the dead.

So, no matter how you feel about the Bible, Jesus still rose from the dead, which means life has a purpose, and Christianity is true.

If you choose to maintain the belief that a resurrection can't occur, then all the evidence in the world won't convice you that a resurrection did occur.

What other evidence is there for the resurrection besides eyewitness testimony?

The empty tomb

One particularly interesting piece of indirect evidence for Jesus' resurrection is the lack of a body or shrine for Jesus despite the fact that He was and is the most famous person in human history.

Jesus was hands down the most impactful person to ever live, leaving a legacy of billions of followers and starting a movement that today nearly a third of the entire population of the world claims to follow. Yet we have no burial place for Him despite the early written records telling us where He was buried.

Let's look at a few interesting points as to how we can be confident that Jesus' tomb was empty.

The resurrection was preached in the same city where Jesus was buried.

Of all the places the message of Jesus' resurrection could have been preached, Jerusalem would have been the worst if the disciples were lying.

The Gospels tell us the entire city was in an uproar over Jesus, and historians, religious leaders, and government officials alike took a keen interest in Jesus when He was alive. To go to the city where Jesus was killed publicly and announce that He wasn't actually dead and that He had risen from the grave would have been crazy if His body was still in the place where it was laid.

The Gospels are very clear as to where Jesus' body was buried, and with all the uproar and the spread of Christianity immediately after His death, it's safe to assume that *someone* would have checked the grave.

At the very least, why preach the message of Jesus' resurrection in the very city He was buried if you weren't certain? That's a recipe for death. Unless, of course, you know you're right.

There were multiple accounts for the empty tomb.

The Bible doesn't have just one source for the empty tomb; it has several. Several people wrote about it and even more saw it. The Gospels and Paul's writings all mention the resurrection and empty tomb.

Dr. Gary Habermas says:

"Scholars think that there could be as many as three or four independent traditions in the Gospels, which very strongly increases the likelihood that the reports are both early and historical."[50]

This is strong evidence because it tells us that this tradition did not arise from one person's experience or perspective. Instead, it came from several different sources.

The earliest Jewish arguments against Christianity admit the empty tomb.

Matthew 28:11-15 tells us that the Jews attempted to refute Christianity by saying that the disciples stole the body.

The Jews did not deny the empty tomb. Their theory that someone stole the body ipso facto admitted that the tomb was empty.

The Toledot Yeshu, a compilation of early Jewish writings, is another source for this. It acknowledges that the tomb was empty and attempts to explain it away.

At least 5 ancient sources state that the Jews admitted the tomb was empty:

1. Early accounts (Acts 13 and 1 Corinthians 15)

2. The Jewish Book - Toledot Yeshu - refers to Jesus and says the tomb was empty but attempts to explain it away by saying His body was removed.

3. Matthew, chapter 28

4. Justin Martyr, an early church father, wrote in AD 150 about this teaching being spread.

5. Tertullian, another early church father, wrote in AD 200 and confirmed what Justin Martyr had said 50 years earlier about the teaching of Jesus' body being removed.

The empty tomb accounts originated within a few years of the event it narrates.

We've already discussed this at great length in previous sections of this book, but the point here is that the New Testament was written much too early in history to have told such a blatant lie if it were such.

The empty tomb is supported by the historical reliability of the burial story.

New Testament scholars agree that the burial story is one of the best-established facts about Jesus due partly to the Gospels identifying Joseph of Arimathea as the one who buried Jesus. Joseph was a member of the Jewish Sanhedrin – a well-known and authoritative ruling class in Jewish society. Because they were well known, it would not be feasible for fictitious stories about them to spread without opposition. If the Christians were lying, they would have been exposed as frauds.

Jesus' tomb was never venerated as a shrine.

The 1st-century custom was to set up a shrine at the site of a holy man's bones, yet there was no such thing set up for Jesus. Since there was no such shrine for Jesus, and considering His fame that continued to grow in and around Jerusalem after His death, the obvious conclusion is that his bones weren't there.

The tomb was discovered empty by women.

As we've discussed, in the 1st century, the testimony of women in Jewish culture was considered to be less valuable and trustworthy than men. So, if the empty tomb story was a legend, it would make sense for male disciples to have discovered it first. Yet women were the chief witnesses to the empty tomb in the Gospels, which means they actually were the first witnesses of the empty tomb.

The Jews and Romans had no motive to steal the body.

The Jews and Romans wanted to end Christianity and restore order. Removing Jesus' body and leaving an empty tomb would not have helped them very much to that end. The disciples had no motive to remove the body, either. They were beaten, killed, and persecuted for preaching about the resurrection. Why would they go through that for a lie?

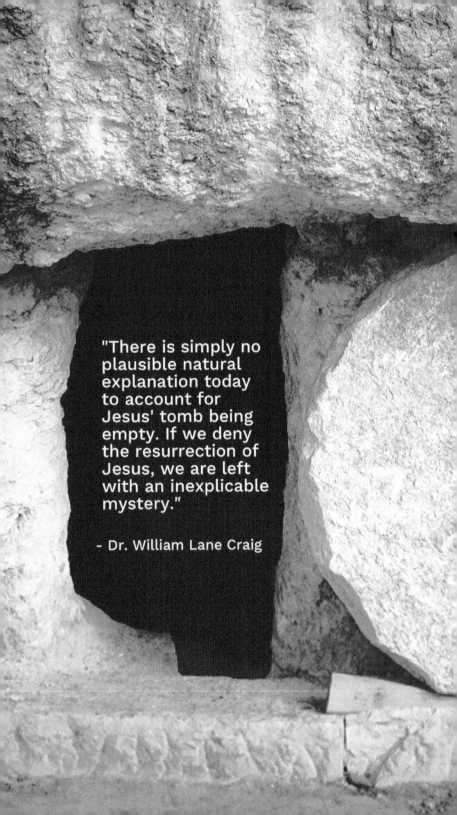

Author Matt Perman writes this about the evidence for the resurrection of Jesus[51]:

> *What explanation, then, do the critics offer, you may ask? [William Lane] Craig tells us that "they are self-confessedly without any explanation to offer. There is simply no plausible natural explanation today to account for Jesus' tomb being empty. If we deny the resurrection of Jesus, we are left with an inexplicable mystery."*

> *Because of the strong evidence for the empty tomb, most recent scholars do not deny it. D.H. Van Daalen has said, "It is extremely difficult to object to the empty tomb on historical grounds; those who deny it do so on the basis of theological or philosophical assumptions." Jacob Kremer, who has specialized in the study of the resurrection and is a NT critic, has said "By far most exegetes hold firmly to the reliability of the biblical statements about the empty tomb" and he lists twenty-eight scholars to back up his fantastic claim.*

We are left with the secure historical conclusion: the tomb was empty, and various 'meetings' took place between Jesus and his followers [...] I regard this conclusion as coming in the same sort of category, of historical probability so high as to be virtually certain, as the death of Augustus in AD 14 or the fall of Jerusalem in AD 70"

- N.T. WRIGHT, NEW TESTAMENT SCHOLAR

Extra-biblical Testimony

According to Dr. Gary Habermas, having two sources for information regarding an ancient historical event is very good.

There are at least 9 ancient non-Christian sources within 150 years of Jesus' life – plus Jewish references after the fact – that all collectively mention Jesus, the apostles, and the events of the New Testament[52]:

1. Tacitus

2. Josephus

3. Suetonius

4. Thallus

5. Phlaegon

6. Pliny the Younger

7. Emperor Trajan

8. Lucian

9. Mara Bar Serapion

10. Jewish religious documents

Add up all of these brief references to Jesus and the apostles, and you get a story that lines up cohesively with the stories about Jesus in the New Testament.

According to J. Warner Wallace, we can learn the following by reading from ancient non-Christian sources:

- Jesus was born and lived in Palestine.

- He was born, supposedly, to a virgin and had an earthly father who was a carpenter.

- He was a teacher who taught that through repentance and belief, all followers would become brothers and sisters.

- He led the Jews away from their beliefs.

- He was a wise man who claimed to be God and the Messiah. He had unusual magical powers and performed miraculous deeds.

- He was persecuted by the Jews for what He said, and He was betrayed.

- He was beaten with rods, forced to drink vinegar, & wore a crown of thorns.

- He was crucified on the eve of the Passover, and this crucifixion occurred under the direction of Pontius Pilate, during the time of Tiberius.

- On the day of His crucifixion, the sky grew dark, and there was an earthquake.

- He was buried in a tomb, and the tomb was later found to be empty.

- He appeared to His disciples resurrected from the grave and showed them His wounds.

- These disciples then told others Jesus was resurrected and ascended into Heaven.

- Jesus' disciples and followers upheld a high moral code.

- The disciples were also persecuted for their faith but were martyred without changing their claims.

- They met regularly to worship Jesus, even after His death.

Wallace says:

> "Not bad, given this information is coming from ancient accounts hostile to the Biblical record. While these non-Christian sources interpret the claims of Christianity differently, they affirm the initial, evidential claims of the Biblical authors (much like those who interpret the evidence related to Kennedy's assassination and the Twin Tower attacks come to different conclusions but affirm the basic facts of the historical events)."[53]

There are at least 9 ancient non-Christian sources within 150 years of Jesus' life that mention Jesus, the apostles, and the events of the New Testament. Together these non-biblical sources give us a story that lines up with the New Testament.

The explosion of the Christian movement after Jesus died

One of the most interesting and compelling pieces of evidence for the resurrection of Jesus is the growth of the early Christian church.

Today and throughout history, movements have spread when an idea resonates with an audience and then delivers on what it promises. The "promise" offered by Christianity was that Jesus rose from the dead, and anyone who followed Him would see greater things than that. That's a lofty promise, yet history shows us continued exponential growth of the movement immediately after Jesus' death.

Rather than speculate about early church growth in terms of the numbers, let's first look at the facts:

Christians were a large enough group by AD 64 (about 30 years after Jesus' death) to be persecuted on a national level in the capital of the Roman Empire. Writings from an early-2nd-century historian named Tacitus tell us that the Roman emperor named Nero, who ruled from 37-68 AD, instituted state-wide persecution based on the belief that Christ-followers had started a giant fire that destroyed much of Rome (also corroborated by another Roman writer named Suetonius).[54]

The torture and hideous deaths of Christians described by Tacitus are appalling, but we can learn a few things from his report of this terrible time in history:

- Christianity had started in Judea and grown enough to move all the way to Rome within 30 years.

- There were enough Christians in Rome in AD 64 to persecute them on a large scale.

Tacitus calls Christians a "class" who were hated and labeled by the "populace." He says after Jesus died, the movement "broke out" in Judaea and "even in Rome."

This description from very early after Jesus' death shows us that Christianity was a sizable and growing movement, and it was all based around the idea that Jesus rose from the dead.

MOVEMENTS SPREAD WHEN AN IDEA DELIVERS ON WHAT IT PROMISES.

It says a lot that Christians were a large enough group within 30 years of Jesus' death to be blamed for a fire and persecuted on a national level in the capital of the Roman Empire. Obviously a LOT of people believed Jesus rose from the dead, and they were willing to be falsely accused, persecuted, and killed for that belief.

People aren't easily drawn into commitment, especially when what you're offering involves committing your entire life to it, and *especially* when you're claiming something as wild as a resurrection from the dead in the very city where this resurrection was said to have happened.

So, if you're a first-century hearer of this message, why would you follow Christianity? The only explanation is that they saw and experienced something worth following - something that lived up to the incredible hype of a man rising from the dead.

The New Testament paints a picture of Jerusalem and the entire surrounding region as being in an uproar over Jesus. Jesus wasn't a man operating in small circles and behind the scenes. He attracted huge crowds for years during His ministry, and He drew the attention of both Jewish and Roman leadership during His life. On a large scale, people knew about Jesus while He was alive, and something compelled them to believe that He rose from the dead.

The Bible says people in the area saw miracles from both Jesus and His followers, and it says large groups of people saw Him resurrected (hundreds, perhaps even the entire city). That's the only explanation for such a large following after Jesus' death.

People are typically very unwilling to experience rejection, discomfort, and pain for something that does not deliver instant personal gratification, yet this early group of Christ-followers jumped head-first into just that. They committed to something outlandish, selfless, and incomprehensible.

Other evidence from the early years of the Christian movement indicates the continued growth of the church, and of course, we know today that within just a few hundred years,

Christianity grew from a hated sect to the official religion of Rome.

Think about it:

This all grew from people who heard a crazy story about a man rising from the dead in the same area they were from, and then they committed to believing it even though it meant they would be looked down on, despised, and abused in all forms because of their decision.

The only rational explanation is that something incredible convinced them.

THE BEST CAUSES REQUIRE <u>COMMITMENT</u>.

LIKE OTHER GREAT MOVEMENTS, FOLLOWING JESUS WASN'T A PASSIVE COMMITMENT.

THIS WASN'T A FEEL-GOOD PHILOSOPHY.

THERE WERE REAL, <u>PAINFUL</u> CONSEQUENCES.

YET HUNDREDS, THOUSANDS, AND EVENTUALLY MILLIONS OF PEOPLE <u>COMMITTED</u> TO IT.

SOMETHING CONVINCED THEM.

WE CAN'T IGNORE THAT.

Did Jesus claim to be God in human form, or did people just give him that label as wishful thinking?

Some say Jesus never meant to be known as God in human form, but instead, certain Jews placed that label on Him due to wishful thinking and the desire for a Messiah.

But there are a few problems with that theory. First, Jesus spoke as if He had the authority to forgive sins (Luke 7:48, Matthew 9:2, Mark 2:5, Luke 5:20).

Then there's the fact that Jesus basically said He was God:

- John 10:30 - "I and the Father are one"

- John 8:58 - "Before Abraham was, I am"

- Matthew, Mark, and Luke - Jesus called Himself the "Son of Man" which is a reference to Daniel 7:13: "In my vision at night I looked, and there before me was one like a son of man, coming with the clouds of heaven. He approached the Ancient of Days and was led into his presence."

Then consider how Jesus seemed to change religious law in an almost casual way:

- Matthew 15:11 - "It is not what enters into the mouth that defiles the man"

- He healed on the Sabbath (Luke 13:16) despite it being forbidden.

Jesus performed miracles, and He said He cast out demons by the finger of God (Luke 11:20). He also said that his miracles of casting out demons signified the coming of the Kingdom of God.

Jesus changed the terms of relating to God by called God "Abba," which means Father, Daddy, or Papa. Mark 14:36 says, "Abba, Father [...] everything is possible for you [...]"

And all of this goes without stating the fact that all through the book of John, Jesus talks as if - and is talked about as - a deity. With all this considered, the answer to the question of whether or not Jesus claimed to be God is very clear. Jesus not only spoke as if He was God in human form, but His actions very clearly communicated the same thing.

What are we left with?

So now we're left with very early reports (that Jesus rose from the dead) from people who all suffered and gave their lives for what they said they saw.

A lot of people give their lives for things, but people are only willing to die for what they genuinely believe to be true.

The disciples were in a position to know if what they believed was actually true. They claimed they actually *saw* the risen Jesus. If it wasn't true, then they dedicated their lives to something they knew was a lie.

If a Christian missionary gives their life today, they're dying for what Peter, John, Paul, James, and the other early disciples claimed to have seen.

But only Peter, John, Paul, James, and the other early disciples died for what they personally believed they *saw* firsthand.

See, giving your life doesn't mean that something is true. But it does mean that you believe it's true. The key is, they *knew* whether or not it was true, and they still willingly gave their lives.

> **If your friends maintain that these are not historical facts, you should ask them what source of information they have that leads them to disagree with over 75% of the trained scholars who have studied this question.**
>
> **- PROFESSOR WILLIAM LANE CRAIG**
> **(REGARDING THE EVIDENCE OF THE RESURRECTION)**

THE EVIDENCE IS OVERWHELMING:

- ⊘ Jesus actually lived.

- ⊘ He did miraculous stuff.

- ⊘ He was crucified.

- ⊘ He rose from the dead.

NO OTHER EXPLANATION FITS THE FACTS.

Why God vs. Science doesn't work

Skeptics might say:

- Science is what started the universe.
- Science is what keeps the universe going.
- Science is the reason the universe exists.

Theists say:

- God is who started the universe.
- God is who keeps the universe going.
- God is the reason the universe exists.

The question is: In the statements above, what's the difference between science and God?

Both viewpoints are looking at the same things:

- The amazing complexity of the universe
- The amazing complexity of life on Earth

In other words, both viewpoints are amazed by how wonderful the world around us is, yet each of them puts a different label on what they see.

That's really the only difference:

One group calls the amazing complexity "science," and the other calls the amazing complexity the handiwork of God.

I've personally been amazed by how comfortable our society is with using labels such as "the universe," "mother nature," "fate," or "destiny." A lot of times, people get uncomfortable with the concept of God, yet they're perfectly okay with appealing to an entity that governs the world around them, just as long as they get to name it something that makes them feel comfortable.

The truth is, we all see the same evidence of something bigger than us in the world around us, and we all call it something. Whether we call it "science," "the universe," or God's creation, it's simply a matter of attribution – it doesn't change reality.

SCIENCE VS GOD

EXACT SAME OBSERVATION, JUST LABELED DIFFERENTLY.

If you look at the world around you at all of the wonders of the universe, namely:

- the vastness of the universe,

- the beauty of the universe,

- the fact that the universe had a beginning,

- the order and complex systems in the universe that keep everything running smoothly,

- the incredibly fine-tuned environment that allows life on Earth,

- the amazing systems within our bodies that allow us to survive and thrive,

- the existence of DNA,

- the existence of intelligence and awareness,

- the existence of emotions like love and hate,

- the existence of creativity,

- the existence of morality,

- and on and on and on,

...and you come to the conclusion that the source of all of those things is an amazing set of elements and processes that come together in an orderly way in a field we call science, how is that any different than simply recognizing that the same set of elements and processes come together in an orderly way through a being called God?

Either way, you're identifying the exact same thing, just through different lenses.

The universe around us is amazing and mind-boggling and mysterious, and we will never have all the answers. So why is it so difficult to simply label our observations as being from God? Labeling our observations as "science" doesn't make those observations any less amazing; it just makes them more confusing when you take God out of the picture.

Our universe is astonishingly orderly and complex, no matter what you believe. Christians simply attribute that complexity to God because they have a scary accurate book that was written thousands of years ago by 40 different writers that tells them that. Why would so many people from so many walks of life go so far out of their way to write a complete lie?

Why doesn't God just physically show us He's real and audibly speak to us?

If God is all-knowing and all-powerful, why doesn't He just come down to Earth, physically reveal Himself, audibly speak to us, and then do some miraculous stuff so we know God is real?

That would completely eliminate any room for doubt, right?

Seems straightforward.

The thing is, God's already tried that, and we killed Him. His name was Jesus.

The truth is, no matter what God does, people will always be able to find a reason to doubt Him. If God came down through the clouds and spoke with a booming voice so the whole world could hear, people would just say they hallucinated it, or someone somehow did it as an elaborate hoax.

But why does God let evil happen? If God is good and God is love, why does He let so much evil go unpunished?

For one, there's the whole free will thing. We have the freedom to make choices, which means we have the ability to mess things up. In order for God to eliminate evil, He would have to eliminate our free will or eliminate us altogether.

Second, we tend to think that when innocent people die, it's the worst thing ever. But if Heaven is real and there's no pain or suffering in Heaven, wouldn't dying just be an upgrade? Wouldn't that be a way of saving them?

Death sucks, but if there really is a Heaven, then dying isn't that bad at all.

God gave human beings the ability to choose. I don't know why, but He did. And human beings make bad choices much of the time (most of the time).

But God has forgiven us for all the bad decisions we're so accustomed to making. He's just giving us time to accept His forgiveness before He comes for us.

Why not listening to Christians because they're biased is just dumb

Saying you can't or shouldn't listen to Christians when it comes to God, the Bible, and Jesus because "they're biased" is more than a little logically flawed. That's a lot like me walking up to you with a brand new pair of shoes on and saying "Man, these are the most comfortable shoes I've ever put on in my life," then you looking at me and saying, "Sorry, I can't believe a word you say because you're biased. After all, you've worn the shoes. I'd rather talk to someone who's never experienced the shoes you're talking about so I can hear what they think about them."

Yet that's what people tend to do with Christianity. They minimize information from Christians simply because they're Christians. But if you want to know how to get somewhere you've never been, it only makes sense to ask people who have been there before. If you want to go to the North Pole, would you ask someone who has never been there for advice on how to get there? Or should you ask someone who has been there, knows the place well, and can tell you all about the journey and how to find your way there?

Bias isn't always a bad thing. And honestly, if Jesus really was who He said He was, shouldn't everyone who came into contact with Him be "biased"? If not, what would that say about His authenticity?

The bottom line is, if you want to know the answers to life's biggest questions, don't listen to people who openly admit that they don't know. Christians may not have it all figured out, but they have a very reliable book that does, and it's been proven to be reliable over thousands of years, and it produces some incredible results.

So, your best bet is to start with that book – the Bible – and talk to the people who know it well. Then make up your own mind and stop listening to the people who simply create confusion when they have absolutely zero information, facts, or evidence to offer to attempt to contradict answers from the Bible.

If you want to go to the
North Pole, it makes
sense to ask someone
who's been there.

If you want to know the
truth about Jesus, it
makes sense to ask
someone who knows Him.

SOMETIMES BIAS IS A GOOD THING.

A few points to hold onto:

The universe had a beginning. What existed before the Big Bang? Nothing? How did the beginning happen, and what caused it?

Life on Earth somehow started from non-life. How did all the right factors come together to create the perfect environment for life?

Once the environment was right for life to happen, what sparked life from non-living matter? How does that even make sense to us?

Once life was sparked from non-living matter, according to modern scientific theories, it somehow survived a long time on Earth without being wiped out. How did life survive on Earth without being wiped out completely, and how is that not a miracle in and of itself?

The universe and life in general have so much order. Where do the laws of physics come from, and why are they there?

Human beings have intelligence, morality, emotions (especially love), and creativity that no other species has.

Why are we so incredibly different from every other living creature? Why are we the only ones who seem to be able to understand how the universe works?

Jesus of Nazareth was a real person, and people really believed they saw Him risen from the dead. What happened with

Jesus? Why would so many people lie about seeing Jesus resurrected and then dedicate their lives to a lie?

What happened to cause the early Christian movement to spread like wildfire within just a few years of Jesus' death? There is very good evidence showing that these early followers all believed that Jesus rose from the dead. That was a pretty radical belief to commit your life to, especially in a society that was already as religious as they were.

The only explanation is that the early believers of Jesus' resurrection (and there were a lot of them) saw and heard compelling proof that convinced them to make such a big commitment and put themselves in the way of ridicule and suffering.

Here's what's important to remember:

- There are really smart people who do not believe in God.

- There are really dumb people who do not believe in God.

- There are really smart people who believe in God.

- There are really dumb people who believe in God.

How do scholars like Bart Ehrman, who believes Christianity is false, and Bruce Metzger, who believes Christianity is true, both very intelligent and well-educated people, see the same evidence yet come to two completely different conclusions?

It seems that intelligence and knowledge of the facts have very little to do with coming to know God.

In other words, no amount of evidence will ever convince you that God is real. You have to be willing to give God a chance to change your heart and then be patient.

(See John 6:44-45, Psalm 34:8, James 1:5, Proverbs 2:6, Proverbs 3:6, Proverbs 8:17, Hebrews 6:5, Psalm 51:6, and Psalm 40:4.)

Facts won't bring you fulfillment.

Facts help lead you to where you're comfortable letting go.

That's faith, and that's where peace and fulfillment are found.

An Important Note on Doubt

Doubt is normal. No matter who you are, you're going to have doubts. It's a part of being human. In fact, even heroes in the Bible had doubts: Job, Abraham, David, Jeremiah, Jewish leaders, John the Baptist, Thomas, and Paul. But for some reason, too many people look down on others for having doubts about God.

I think most atheists believe in God in some form or fashion. They just don't know Him as well as they would like to, so they label themselves as atheists while they try to figure it out. In fact, some atheists will openly tell you that they're angry with God, and you can't be angry with someone you don't believe in.

In his book *The Thomas Factor*, Dr. Gary Habermas says there are 3 types of doubt: factual or philosophical doubt, emotional doubt, and volitional doubt.[55]

According to Habermas, most people doubt for emotional reasons. That's the largest group of doubters (70-85% of all doubters).

Sometimes doubt is helpful, and sometimes it's not, but doubt in-and-of-itself is not negative. Doubt is also not a sin. God can handle your questions. There are many passages where biblical believers not only doubted God, but they also reached the point of downright lashing out at Him.

You're going to doubt no matter who you are. The question, then, is not *if* you doubt, but whether or not you know what to do about your doubts. If you don't know what to do about your doubts, you'll end up floating back and forth and being tossed around by the latest trends and ideas.

It's important to know that doubts are almost never remedied by information. According to Dr. Habermas, only about 15% of doubts are factual. Sure, dealing with factual doubts is important, but there's more than enough evidence to get you past those doubts.

In other words, good answers are necessary, but not sufficient. They simply serve as the foundation for faith.

Let's look a little closer at the different types of doubt.

Doubts are almost never remedied by information.

Good answers are necessary, but not sufficient.

They simply serve as a foundation

for faith.

Factual Doubt

Dr. Habermas says doubts about God are most common from age 18 to early 30s, and the majority of young people say they walk away from their faith in a secular school. Many of them come back in their early 30s, but that's approximately a decade of the most productive years of their lives gone.

A lot of the time, their confusion comes from a professor or someone else dismissing and belittling Christians. These people don't typically give refutations; they just dismiss it and belittle it. They tend to apply peer pressure to young people and make them feel as if intellectual people don't believe in things like Jesus.

The biggest reasons young people doubt are typically:

1. They're being pressured by their peers.

2. They're caught up in some type of negative behavior they either don't want to address or don't want to give up.

3. They get lost in their emotions.

The thing is, even though college experiences are known for challenging religious ideologies, college professors don't typically refute Christianity. If they do, they'll use a poor refutation.

They might say something like:

"Did you know there were multiple crucified and risen saviors prior to Jesus?"

They might point to others who were also born on December 25th and say they were also crucified and risen. They might try to make them feel like churches or messiahs are not unique.

But there were no crucified and risen saviors before Jesus. The main "messiahs" skeptics point to never lived and therefore were never crucified and risen. According to Dr. Habermas, even agnostic scholar Bart Ehrman says that's all garbage.

The problem is, people usually don't separate central versus peripheral doctrines. Periphery doctrines are the things that atheists like Bill Maher love to use to belittle Christians. They focus on the little details like eschatology.

The two most common beliefs Christians lose when challenged is:

#1: Someone challenges them by saying something like the universe wasn't created in six 24-hour days.

The answer should be: "And? Your point?"

Or...

#2: Someone tells them the Bible is not inerrant (in other words, it's filled with errors).

The answer should be: "Your point?" They might say, "That means you can't believe it," but that does not follow.

Even if you believe the majority of the Bible is unreliable, you can still use the parts of the Bible even skeptics accept as historically accurate documents and still show that the resurrection occurred.

I personally don't believe there are mistakes in the Bible, but even if there *were* mistakes in the details, I could still hold my doctrines because Christianity is based on the truth of the gospel data.

If all that's true about Christianity is that Jesus is the Son of God who died on the cross for our sins and was raised from the dead, then Christianity follows.

And it just so happens that the strongest evidence we have is for Jesus being the Son of God who died on the cross for our sins and was raised from the dead.

Just remember: People will always debate 6-day creation and all the other details in the Bible, but those are periphery issues. They're small details in comparison to the primary message of the Bible.

You can't have the mindset that if one thing in the Bible is confusing or doesn't seem to make sense, then the Bible as a whole can't be right in any area at all. That's not logical.

I'm convinced the Bible is 100% correct, but human beings have an overwhelming tendency to misinterpret and argue over things. It's what we do.

The gospel message (that Jesus is the Son of God, He died on the cross for our sins, and He was raised from the dead so that we could have life) is one thing in the Bible that is absolutely undeniable.

It also just so happens to be the most important thing in the entire Bible, and it's the one doctrine that is the most supported by evidence. In other words, God put the most evidence for the most important thing we need to know.

The gospel isn't all there is to the Bible, but in the Bible itself, Paul clearly put "first importance" on the gospel (1 Corinthians 15:3).

So, Christians are most defensible in their most important belief. Everything else people love to argue over is just periphery and a distraction from the central information.

Ask yourself this: How much would it change your life and eternal future if [insert Christian doctrine] were true? How much would it change your life and eternal future if it were false?

For example, if you found out tomorrow that the world was created in 6 literal days instead of 6 long time periods, how would that affect your life, purpose, and future? The truth is, it wouldn't at all. Because regardless of whether you're right or wrong about your periphery doctrines, Jesus Christ still lived, died, and rose from the dead for you to have true life in relationship with God. That's what matters.

Minimize the importance you place on periphery issues. It will save you a lot of stress and wasted time.

Was Calvin wrong? What if he was? And? What follows from that? That Calvin was wrong? So what?

Look to answer the most important central doctrines:

- Jesus is the Son of God.

- Jesus died on the cross for our sins.

- Jesus was resurrected from the dead.

Then, if that's not working and something is still nagging at you, and you're in pain, then you're probably experiencing emotional doubt.

GETTING LOST IN THE DETAILS

Christianity has the most evidence for the most important aspect - Jesus' resurrection. But more often than not, it's the small details that cause people to leave their faith. Focus on what's most important - Jesus' resurrection - and let other people argue over 6-day creation and church music.

DO NOT LET THE PERIPHERY DISTRACT YOU FROM WHAT'S MOST IMPORTANT.

Emotional Doubt

According to Dr. Habermas, emotional doubt is the most painful, but it's the least serious.

In fact, emotional doubt is the only doubt that comes with pain. Factual doubt and volitional doubt don't hurt, but emotional doubt does.

Emotional doubters know the facts; they just have a hard time believing them due to an emotional view of the facts. They might think it's too good to be true, or they might obsess over all the "what if's" that they ultimately can't answer anyway.

When you have the facts of a situation, but you still struggle with doubt, there's probably an emotional, anxious, or obsessive cause to those doubts.

Emotional doubters usually ask similar questions to factual doubters, but they ask for different reasons.

For example, they might both ask for evidence of the resurrection, but one is genuinely looking for facts they don't have, and the other is asking because they're really wondering if it could be possible to be wrong.

Habermas says that one common characteristic of emotional doubt is when a question starts with "What if...".

The person asking a question like that probably knows the evidence, but they often wonder things like, "What if we're wrong?"

But you could turn that around and say, "Do you have any reason to think we're wrong?"

People with emotional doubt tend to have general "what if" questions without evidence behind it. Their doubt is painful. They might say things like, "It would be *horrible* to be wrong."

They might have fears about Jesus saying He never knew them or that they might still go to hell even though they're saved. They might also obsess over questions like, "How do I know if I love God?" and other questions that can't be backed by evidence.

Most of the time in our lives, it's not the facts of the situations around us that are important; it's how we process those facts. Similarly, the worst kind of pain in our lives is not from what happens to us but how we download it or process it.

Dr. Habermas says emotional doubters might include people who keep getting saved because they doubt their salvation. They just "know" they're not saved even though they believe the gospel. It's an emotional response to the data.

For these people, when something bad happens, they give themselves permission to let those events determine why they have problems. However, beliefs (i.e., the way we download information) are the things that stand between those events that happen to us and the consequences that come from them.

Events alone rarely cause all the consequences we experience. Events plus negative or detrimental beliefs about those events often cause excessive consequences. So, when we say negative things to ourselves about things that matter to us – things like "What if God doesn't really love me?" – it's important to refute those thoughts with "That's not true because..."

It's all about how you talk to yourself about the events in your life because most of us lie to ourselves without even realizing it. Here are 3 steps to dealing with this type of emotionally driven thought pattern:

First, locate the misbelief. Usually, there's a primary and secondary misbelief. You might say one lie to yourself, but there's usually a deeper lie about life beneath that. Then remove and replace it by reminding yourself, "That's not true because…" Replace the misbelief with a proven truth. Change your perspective, pray, celebrate God, and see things from His perspective instead of from the negative, misleading perspective.

After all, most emotional doubters are anxious doubters. They're being anxious or obsessive-compulsive by doubting. It's not a rational issue they're dealing with.

An example of emotional doubt might be someone who has no problem believing that God exists, but emotionally they can't come to grips with why God would allow evil to come into their lives. They've seen the facts, and the facts make sense, but they let their emotions dictate what they're willing to believe.

DO YOU <u>THINK</u> GOD'S NOT THERE OR ARE YOU <u>AFRAID</u> GOD'S NOT THERE?

Most of the damage that occurs in our lives is not from what happens to us, but how we process it. That's why thinking the worst about every situation is a very poisonous thing to do.

It's okay to doubt, just be sure that you're being honest with yourself about why you're doubting. Do you really think God's not there or are you afraid God's not there? Those are two totally different things, but both can be overcome.

A lot of times, this type of person has moved past the intellectual stage of doubting and into emotional doubting. They see the world the way it is, they've heard the explanation of why it is that way, yet they don't want to believe it.

The emotional doubter might say, "But what about hell? What is it, and who goes there? And how can it exist with a loving God?" These are questions that go beyond available human knowledge and therefore require faith.

You must address emotional doubts before giving up and completely turning off to God. That's what Dr. Habermas calls volitional doubt.

Volitional doubt describes people who know Christianity is true, but they're mad at God, and they've turned away from God completely.

The good news is, you're in control of your doubts. You get to decide what to do with them and how to manage them.

What should we do with doubt?

First of all, remember that the most damage that occurs in our lives is not from what happens to us but how we process it. That's why saying or thinking negative things to ourselves is a very poisonous thing to do.

So, understanding the necessary facts is key, but then reminding yourself of those facts in negative situations is also vital. After all, the facts about God don't change just because your circumstances change.

But where does faith come into all of this?

In Scripture, the word for "hope" refers to a grounded hope, not a hope in something you don't know about. That hope comes from faith that is grounded in facts.

Faith is not a weak sister that you add to the heavy stuff – science, history, philosophy, etc. Faith does what reason can't do. Faith says, "This can be trusted." Faith says, "Quit asking 'what if' about stupid questions when you already have good answers. Otherwise, you're going to be hurting."

Reason says, "Here are good responses." Faith says, "Those are good enough. You can trust those. Walk in it." Faith comes along and says that belief is warranted.

Faith is trusting the evidence.

It's okay to keep studying to build on good answers, but not because you have to keep answering the same question every day.

You have to train the habit of faith. Learn the art of learning enough and then letting go.

And faith is not going to stay there if you ignore it. That's why people who follow Jesus read the Bible, worship, fellowship with other Christians, etc. because it reinforces our faith when we hang around people who don't think they have to answer the same questions every day.

Facts say, "This can be trusted."

Faith says, "Quit asking questions."

Nothing is certain, so get the facts and then let go.

So, what are you putting your faith in?

Faith is a process.

Faith is a process. It's not something you instantly gain once you hear the facts.

It's important to hear the facts first, but the facts can't answer every question for you. So, once you have all the pertinent facts, you have to choose to move past your emotions and trust in something outside of your understanding. That's what faith is. After all, isn't that what we do in every area of our lives anyway?

You don't know for a fact that every single component of your vehicle is intact and working properly, yet you drive it anyways. You don't know for a fact that every single piece and part holding your house or apartment together is in good shape and capable of carrying its load, but you still go home and walk inside.

You aren't certain that when you go to sleep, your body will continue working flawlessly, and yet you still fall asleep.

Many doubts we face about God simply come down to the fact that our worldviews have a hard time changing. For some of us, that's a much larger stretch than for others, but it's 100% possible to get there.

The important thing to remember is this:

Get the most important facts on God, the Bible, Jesus, and the resurrection. Once you have those facts, decide to take the leap of faith. To do this, you have to reach a place where you understand the most important facts well enough to know that they're compelling at the very least and are therefore worth the leap.

After you've decided to trust God, the process of aligning your worldview to God's worldview begins. Doubts will periodically come in, and when they do, go back to the truths that are in this book, the Bible, and the notes that you wrote down. Your mind will forget them, so regularly remind yourself of them. Then pray to God and ask Him for help. He WILL help you.

So, prepare for doubts about God. They're normal, and the good news is, they're irrational. Knowing that and then replacing irrational thoughts with factual truth about God will help you get past the doubts and into a place of hope and joy.

Closing Thoughts

I hope this book has encouraged you and shown you that there are good reasons to have confident faith in Jesus Christ. I hope that you're now able to see the world around you in a different light and through a lens of hope and purpose.

Whether you've spent your life in church or never heard of Jesus before, I want you to know that you did not come into existence as a result of chaos, and your life is not accidental. There's a purpose in everything around you, everything that came before you, and everything that will come after you. Regardless of your background or current situation, we all lose sight of that from time to time, but I hope you've seen in this book that nature itself speaks of that truth, and Jesus Christ confirms it.

I want you to walk away from this book knowing that there is more. So often in our lives, we settle for what's readily available, comfortable, or easy to accept. I hope this book has pushed you outside of your comfort zone enough to make you think deeper and more intentionally about your life than you have before.

The truth is, we're all going to have to address this sooner or later. It doesn't have to be sad or morbid; it's just a reality. We're all going to die, and *something's* going to happen immediately afterward. You're either going to cease to exist, or you're going to meet the Creator of the Universe. In this book, we've gone over some *very* good evidence that says, beyond a reasonable doubt, that you're meeting God the moment after you die. If there's even a remote chance of that being true, why would you not devote your time and energy to living in light of that fact?

But this is not just about where you go after you die. Too many of us live mundane, meaningless, and passionless lives because we're not confident about why we're here. But once you realize that God is not just an idea to make you feel better about where you go when you die, then you can start to experience the life He designed you for here on Earth. You were never meant to simply go through the motions and get by. You were made to live a fulfilled and passionate life, and that life is waiting for you to take hold of it as soon as you realize that it's true.

Imagine someone writing you a billion-dollar check. They make it out to you, sign it, and hand it to you. If you don't know the person that wrote the check, then you might not cash it. After all, what if it's not real? What if it's a scam? You might be skeptical and think, "Why am I receiving this in the first place?" It's likely that you'll think it's too good to be true. Without realizing the truth behind the gift, you'll never access its value.

But if you take time to look at the facts about the person who gave you the gift, then eventually you'll understand the situation and trust them enough to cash the check and spend the money. And a gift of that magnitude can forever change your life – if you'll only access it.

Your life is in that very situation every moment of every day. You're given a gift each day you wake up and each moment after that. What will you do with it? Will you look at the facts about the Gift-Giver to see that He's worth trusting? Once you've seen enough evidence to establish that fact, will you trust Him and accept what's been given to you?

If so, choose to trust Jesus. Ask Him to walk with you and guide you. It's that simple. Then, submit to the process and don't get frustrated when you can't understand things. Just adjust your focus to what you see and know to be true. Come back to this book if you need to. Remind yourself of the truth about who God is, who you are because of Him, and why you're here.

Faith is a journey, not a destination. So, whether you're a lifelong Christian, an atheist, or anywhere in-between, we all need perspective. That's what this book is about. Perspective adjusts our focus, and we all need an adjustment from time to time to get back to what's most important. Your career, family, friends, and finances are important, but they're not what's most important.

We all get distracted, but I hope this book has shown you that you're here for much more than it may seem when you're in the middle of the day-to-day grind. There's evidence all around us that speaks to that truth, and hopefully, you're able to see that more clearly now.

If I could leave you with one thought, it would be this: Continue to open your mind to why you're here, explore the evidence in front of you, then trust what you can't see. That's where fulfillment and hope are found, and I pray that you receive that and walk in it every day of your life going forward. God bless.

If you have further questions, or if this book has helped you in any way, connect with me at mikeptaylor.net or email me at mike@mikeptaylor.net.

References

[1] https://www.pewforum.org/2018/04/25/when-americans-say-they-believe-in-god-what-do-they-mean/

[2] https://www.apa.org/monitor/2019/01/numbers

[3] See reasons.org, specifically
https://www.reasons.org/explore/publications/rtb-101/read/rtb-101/2012/01/13/is-there-evidence-for-the-big-bang

[4] See Mythbusters: God and Science video with Dr. Hugh Ross -
https://youtu.be/LcGX_6AiHKI

[5] https://www.scientificamerican.com/article/15-answers-to-creationist/

[6] https://wmap.gsfc.nasa.gov/universe/uni_age.html

[7] https://www1.cbn.com/cbnnews/us/2017/august/a-cosmos-divinely-designed-for-life-reasons-to-believe

[8] Also see reasons.org/fine-tuning

[9] https://www.space.com/11642-dark-matter-dark-energy-4-percent-universe-panek.html

[10] https://science.nasa.gov/astrophysics/focus-areas/what-is-dark-energy

[11] See Genesis 1:1, Genesis 2:3-4, Psalm 148:5, Isaiah 42:5, Isaiah 45:18, John 1:3, Col. 1:15-17, Isaiah 40:26, Hebrews 11:3

[12] The information in this section is from various lectures from Dr. Frank Turek.

[13] https://crossexamined.org/god-and-the-astronomers/

[14] See Jastrow's book *God and the Astronomers*

[15] Stephen Hawking, *A Brief History of Time*

[16] Richard Dawkins, *The Blind Watchmaker*, p. 116

[17] The information in this section is from various lectures from Dr. Frank Turek.

[18] Norman L. Geisler, Frank Turek, *I Don't Have Enough Faith to Be an Atheist*, p. 142

[19] Francis S. Collins, director of the Human Genome Project, The Language of God, (Free Press, New York, NY), 2006

[20] Francis S. Collins, *The Language of God*, p 3.

[21] This section comes from a lecture from Dr. Stephen Meyer titled Philosopher of Science Stephen C. Meyer Explores The Exciting Theory of Intelligent Design - https://youtu.be/tu93Mw4mtec

[22] Michael J. Behe, *Darwin's Black Box: The Biochemical Challenge to Evolution*

[23] See video titled "Ben Stein vs. Richard Dawkins Interview" - https://youtu.be/GlZtEjtlirc

[24] See reasons.org/fine-tuning for more information

[25] Read Why the Universe Is The Way It Is for more information.

[26] See "In the blink of an eye" - http://news.mit.edu/2014/in-the-blink-of-an-eye-0116

[27] See "Anatomy of the Eye" - https://www.umkelloggeye.org/conditions-treatments/anatomy-eye

[28] http://sciencespeaks.dstoner.net/Christ_of_Prophecy.html

[29] This section comes from a lecture from Dr. Hugh Ross titled "Mythbusters: God and Science - Part 1" - https://youtu.be/LcGX_6AiHKI

[30] http://www.hawking.org.uk/the-beginning-of-time.html

[31] Lawrence Krauss, *A Universe from Nothing*, p. 173

[32] The information in this section about Biblical and scientific alignment is based on and adapted from http://www.clarifyingchristianity.com/science.shtml#001.

[33] See web page on University of California, Santa Barbara's website titled "About how many stars are in space?" - https://scienceline.ucsb.edu/getkey.php?key=3775

[34] https://www.npr.org/sections/krulwich/2012/09/17/161096233/which-is-greater-the-number-of-sand-grains-on-earth-or-stars-in-the-sky

[35] http://curious.astro.cornell.edu/for-teachers/78-the-universe/stars-and-star-clusters/general-questions/353-are-all-stars-the-same-beginner

[36] See "The Discovery of the Weight of the Air" - https://doi.org/10.1038/078294a0

[37] https://pmm.nasa.gov/education/water-cycle/hydrologic-cycle

[38] https://www.weather.gov/jetstream/ll_h2ocontent

[39] https://www.bbc.com/future/article/20190503-the-deepest-hole-we-have-ever-dug

[40] See article titled "Early Earth was covered in a global ocean and had no mountains" at https://www.newscientist.com/article/2130266-early-earth-was-covered-in-a-global-ocean-and-had-no-mountains/ and "A Cool Early Earth" at https://nai.nasa.gov/media/medialibrary/2013/10/Cooler-Early-Earth-Article.pdf

[41] See video titled "Agnostic Scholar The Myth of Jesus" - https://youtu.be/r87w6eO7nJw

[42] See video titled "Did Jesus Exist? Atheist Bart Ehrman Explains" - https://youtu.be/2SyPPhwNfqQ

[43] This section comes from Cold Case Christianity's website - http://coldcasechristianity.com/2015/why-i-know-the-gospels-were-written-early-free-bible-insert/

[44] See video titled "The Resurrection Argument That Changed a Generation of Scholars" - https://youtu.be/ay_Db4RwZ_M

[45] See article titled "Testing the Gospels From John to Hippolytus" - https://coldcasechristianity.com/writings/testing-the-gospels-from-john-to-hippolytus/

[46] McGrath JJ, Saha S, Al-Hamzawi A, et al. Psychotic Experiences in the General Population: A Cross-National Analysis Based on 31 261 Respondents From 18 Countries. JAMA Psychiatry. 2015;72(7):697–705. doi:10.1001/jamapsychiatry.2015.0575 - http://jamanetwork.com/journals/jamapsychiatry/fullarticle/2298236

[47] Quote from Dartmouth about hallucinations not occurring in healthy people without psychological disorders - https://sites.dartmouth.edu/dujs/2009/11/21/hallucination-a-normal-phenomenon/)

[48] See https://www.ncbi.nlm.nih.gov/pmc/articles/PMC3827523/

[49] https://my.clevelandclinic.org/health/diseases/17373-pleural-effusion-causes-signs--treatment

[50] See article titled "The Empty Tomb of Jesus" at https://www.namb.net/apologetics-blog/the-empty-tomb-of-jesus/

[51] See article titled "Historical Evidence for the Resurrection" - https://www.desiringgod.org/articles/historical-evidence-for-the-resurrection

[52] See "Chapter IX Ancient Non-Christian Sources" from *The Historical Jesus* at garyhabermas.com/books/historicaljesus/historicaljesus.htm#ch9

[53] See article titled "Is There Any Evidence for Jesus Outside the Bible?" at https://coldcasechristianity.com/writings/is-there-any-evidence-for-jesus-outside-the-bible/

[54] See *The Annals* (Book XV) - http://classics.mit.edu/Tacitus/annals.11.xv.html

[55] See video titled "Dealing with Factual Doubt - Dr. Gary Habermas" which is part 1 of 4 in the lecture series - https://youtu.be/zASo5K9dZtQ

Grounded Faith for Practical People

The Simple Visual Guide to Confident Faith

Made in the USA
Coppell, TX
07 February 2020

15511046R00128